The Soul of the First Amendment

The Soul of
the First
Amendment

Floyd Abrams

Yale UNIVERSITY PRESS

New Haven & London

Published with assistance from the foundation established in memory
of Philip Hamilton McMillan of the Class of 1894, Yale College.

Yale University Press books may be purchased in quantity for educa-
tional, business, or promotional use. For information, please e-mail
sales.press@yale.edu (US office) or sales@yaleup.co.uk (UK office).

Set in Janson Roman type by Integrated Publishing Solutions.
Printed in the United States of America.

Library of Congress Control Number: 2016950165
ISBN 978-0-300-19088-5 (hardcover : alk. paper)
ISBN 978-0-300-23420-6 (pbk.)

A catalogue record for this book is available from the British Library.

10 9 8 7 6 5 4 3 2 1

For Efrat

The very reason for the First Amendment is to make the people of the country free to think, speak, write and worship as they wish, not as the Government commands.

—Justice Hugo Black

Contents

Acknowledgments   ix

Introduction   xiii

The Soul of the First Amendment   1

Index   139

Acknowledgments

This book is one of ruminations about certain aspects of American constitutional law that have long been of special interest to me—the uniqueness of American First Amendment–rooted law protecting "the freedom of speech and of the press"; the degree to which democratic nations —Canada and the United States, for example—that share so many values to such an extraordinary degree nonetheless veer in different directions when the protection of speech is involved; and the difficult, sometimes painful decision-making process that American and other journalists and commentators engage in (or that I think they should engage in) about what to say when law imposes few barriers to their saying just about anything they choose.

Acknowledgments

While I've thought about such matters for some time, the process of preparing even a short book has required the substantial assistance and often the forbearance of many people. I start with my dear wife of fifty-three years, Efrat, who encouraged me to write the book even if it led to my absence from our home for more than a few weekends. I thank my associate Celia Belmonte for all her assistance in finding certain materials and in analyzing them all. I thank my partner Susan Buckley and Professor Catherine J. Ross for reading the manuscript and offering their reactions to it. All views in the book and, of course, all errors are mine alone.

I thank my inestimable assistant Denise O'Neill for protecting me from much of the turmoil of day-to-day life and encouraging me to complete the task of authorship. I thank my agent Karen Gantz for her counsel, her dedication to the book's creation, and her continuing encouragement in its drafting. I thank Marcy Lovitch for typing much of the book on the many Sundays I spent in my office writing it. And I thank my partners and associates at Cahill Gordon & Reindel for all the conversations and discussions I have had with them throughout the years about the topic of the book and just about everything else.

Acknowledgments

I am delighted that Yale University Press is publishing the book and want to offer particular thanks to Steve Wasserman, who oversaw the book from its earliest days of conception.

Introduction

In 1976, my wife and I and our two children traveled across the Atlantic Ocean to England on the QE2. Among the many amenities offered on the ship were current movies, one of which was *All the President's Men*, which showed how *Washington Post* reporters Bob Woodward and Carl Bernstein exposed the Watergate scandal that led to the resignation of President Richard Nixon. The movie received a number of Oscars, including one for William Goldman, the picture's screenwriter. In addition to writing such unforgettable lines as "Follow the money," Goldman included occasional curse words uttered by the journalists and others. The movie received a PG rating in the

United States and, because of its use of profanity, a more restrictive one in Britain.

My son, Dan, was then ten and wanted to see the movie. When he tried to enter the ship's theater, he was stopped by an officious English steward and told that because of his age and the movie's British rating, he could not do so. Dan argued for a while and then, as he turned away from the guard, muttered, "That's why we had a revolution. That's why we have a First Amendment." When he returned to our cabin and told me the story, I beamed.

Of course, as my son learned long before he entered Columbia Law School, the First Amendment applies only to the government and not to private entities such as the Cunard Line. But he was on to something, and that was the spirit of the First Amendment, its anticensorial soul.

This essay is about that soul—freedom of speech—why it matters and, as a result, how different American society is from other Western democratic states. The First Amendment is a mere forty-five words: *"Congress shall make no law respecting an establishment of religion, or prohibiting the free exercise thereof; or abridging the freedom of speech or of the press; or the right of the people peaceably to assemble, and to petition the Government for a redress of grievances."* That's it. Because of the adoption of post–Civil War amendments to the Constitution and subsequent judicial interpretation of them, the First Amendment also applies to the states. And it applies as well to the president and other federal officials and to other governmental entities—cities, towns, and municipalities and their employees.

This modest essay focuses on the nine words that bar the government from "abridging the freedom of speech or of the press," and on the interpretation of that language by the Supreme Court. I do so largely by comparing American law and practice on this topic to the laws governing free speech in other democratic nations. I do this not to bestow some sort of First Amendment valentine on the United States but to explore the nature of the differences in approach in this contentious arena. After all, American First Amendment law, former United States solicitor general and associate justice of the Supreme Judicial Court of Massachusetts Charles Fried has rightly said, "is the most libertarian and speech protective of any liberal democratic regime." As such, its consequences and implications are profound.

The exceptionalism of the United States in the protections it offers to freedom of expression does not mean that other democratic nations do not respect, honor, and generally seek to protect it; it does mean that American law does so more often, more intensely, and more controversially than is true elsewhere. Nor, to put it another way, does it mean that the United States cares less than other democratic nations do about a bevy of competing interests such as the vice of discrimination, the need for equality, the harm that defamation can do to personal reputation, the significance of personal privacy, and the need to safeguard national security. It does mean, however, that although American law seeks to protect those interests, it does so only after weighing, with far greater concern than occurs elsewhere, the dangers of government interference with and control over free expression.

The uniquely high level of American protection for free expression does not necessarily mean that American society is better served in all respects. I think that is generally so, but one could hardly argue that Canada, whose approach to such matters is in many ways similar to that of democratic Europe, suffers under a yoke of repression as a result.

Nevertheless, adopting a legal system that defends speech in a less exuberant manner than the United States has consequences. For example, in Canada and throughout Europe, what is commonly referred to as "hate speech"—attacks on people or groups based on race, religion, or national origin—is illegal in a variety of circumstances. In Belgium, for instance, a member of the parliament was found guilty of a crime for distributing leaflets urging, among other things, "Stand Up against the Islamification of Belgium." In England, a man was convicted of committing a similar crime for carrying a poster saying "Islam out of Britain—Protect the British People." The European Court of Human Rights affirmed both convictions, ruling that they did not violate the European Convention on Human Rights.

In the United States, as Donald Trump's recent campaign for the presidency illustrated, such statements, whatever their level of offense, are unequivocally protected by the First Amendment. Trump's verbal castigation of Muslims and Mexicans were among the centerpieces of his quest for the Republican nomination. In Europe, such language would have provided a basis for criminal charges to be filed against him. In addition, statements denouncing homosexuals, Jews, Catholics, and other minority groups are the basis for criminal prosecutions in many democratic nations. By contrast, in the United States, such speech is routinely protected by the First Amendment.

There is no doubt that a price is paid, sometimes a serious one, for doing so; the American approach is not oblivious to that price but insists (as other countries do not) that the dangers of permitting the government to decide what may and may not be said, far more often than not, outweigh any benefits that may result from suppressing or punishing offensive speech.

Consider another example: throughout Europe, in an effort to protect the privacy of individuals who were involved in newsworthy events of the past that are no longer considered of relevance at this time, a "right to be forgotten" has been adopted that requires entities such as Google, at the request of the individuals involved, to remove links to previously published material that refers to them. As a result, published descriptions of many events of the past that were widely and truthfully reported on, including public judicial proceedings, are unavailable throughout Europe via Google. So far, Google has removed links to more than five hundred thousand previously published articles. Thus, the law's proponents believe, compelling privacy interests are protected. Why, European law asks, must a victim of no current public note of a crime from years ago or even the perpetrator of a little-recalled crime of yesteryear be defined today by a Google summary of their past pain or misconduct? How, American law responds, can a government be permitted to ban the disclosure of truthful information about matters of public interest of the past without assaulting history itself?

This essay is divided into six brief chapters. The first is primarily historical in nature, tracing the debates over ratification of the Constitution as originally drafted without any First Amendment or other provision of the Bill of Rights. It concludes that the central purpose of the First Amendment was to impose strict limits on governmental authority over religion, speech, and press and that recent arguments, primarily by liberal jurists and scholars, to the contrary are unpersuasive. It offers a look at life in the United States until well into the twentieth century, a period during which the First Amendment was virtually invisible. So slight a role did it then play that the United States of a hundred years ago would be virtually unrecognizable to anyone today who was transported back to that time, a time a few years before socialists (including presidential candidate Eugene V. Debs) would be imprisoned for their opposition to America's participation in the First World War. So insignificant a role did the First Amendment then play that a novel such as *Ulysses* could not be legally sold in the United States until the 1930s and criticism of the judiciary was subject to stern sanctions until the 1940s. So hidden was the authority of the First Amendment that not a single act of Congress was held unconstitutional under it until 1965.

The second chapter compares the extraordinary level of legal protection afforded to speech in the United States with that of other countries. The constitutionally required tolerance for hate speech is one example. Others include the far greater use of libel and privacy law in nations that lack the constraining force of a First Amendment and the far more stringent limitations on such claims in the United States.

The third chapter describes a seminal but too-little-recalled First Amendment case decided in 1941, one that decisively rejected English law as a guide for the United States. While that case, *Bridges v. California*, dealt specifically with free speech as it related to courts and judges, its impact has been great and wide-ranging, setting America on the path of providing far more legal protection for free expression than exists or has ever existed elsewhere.

The fourth and fifth chapters examine two areas in which American law deviates with particular clarity and impact from laws applied elsewhere: the so-called right to be forgotten and the controversial body of law that provides First Amendment protection for unlimited spending by individuals and corporations in political campaigns, rulings that are contrary to those in other democratic nations.

The sixth and final chapter deals with issues that law alone cannot resolve and that may be still more controversial than the legal ones. They include how, given all the protections for freedom of speech in the United States, free speech should be responsibly exercised. What, for example, are we to make of Edward Snowden's and Julian Assange's acts and revelations? How should journalists respond to the availability of highly classified materials? What internal limitations do and should journalists place on what they publish? How should they respond to government requests or demands that they refrain from publishing certain materials? Such issues are notoriously easier to ask than to answer, and I offer my own views about them in chapter VI.

In a previous book, I quoted a passage that George Orwell wrote in one of his newspaper columns. It is worth repeating here as a way of emphasizing that there is a limit to the impact of written words in any constitution, a point I emphasize later in the book. This is what Orwell wrote: "If large numbers of people are interested in freedom of speech, there will be freedom of speech, even if the law forbids it; if public opinion is sluggish, inconvenient minorities will be persecuted, even if laws exist to protect them."

The statement was obviously limited to democratic nations. In nations where journalists are jailed or worse for engaging in what all democratic nations view as freedom of expression, public opinion is of far less significance. The free-speech protective language of constitutions in those nations is simply a collection of lies.

Orwell also should not be read to minimize the differences between living in a nation with a First Amendment and one without one. It was not happenstance that led the *Guardian*, an English publication, to prepare and initially print all of its Snowden-rooted stories through its American arm. As Alan Rusbridger, the *Guardian*'s editor, put it, "America has its own difficulties with journalists and their sources. But it is, nonetheless, a kinder environment for anyone trying to inform the sort of public debate regarding security and privacy that, post-Snowden at least, everyone seems to agree is desirable. A written constitution, the First Amendment, and the Supreme Court judgment in the Pentagon Papers case in 1971 have all played their part in establishing protections that are lacking in the UK."

Orwell's comment is not inconsistent with this legal reality. First Amendment law is critical in defending freedom of expression. But so, as Orwell recognized, is public opinion. A country that honors freedom of speech is far more likely to protect it than one that does not. And as my then-so-youthful son illustrated forty years ago, the First Amendment is part of this country's ethos, its popular culture, unrivaled by any other provision in the Constitution.

When President Franklin Delano Roosevelt delivered a celebrated radio address to the nation early in 1941, he offered a vision of a postwar world that would be guided by four principles. The speech came to be known as the Four Freedoms Speech and the first was freedom of speech. When the artist Norman Rockwell attended a town meeting in Vermont later that year and saw a single person rise and speak in opposition to a popular proposal to build a new school, he was struck by the respect with which all who attended the meeting gave to the dissenting citizen. Rockwell painted a picture showing the man speaking as others in the meeting carefully listened. He called the painting *Freedom of Speech*. He then painted three more relating to the other freedoms listed by Roosevelt in his speech—freedom of worship, freedom from want, and freedom from fear. Each appeared on the cover of the *Saturday Evening Post*, and each has been widely displayed ever since throughout the country.

Two of the four freedoms so celebrated are to be found in the First Amendment, and it is no exaggeration to say that principles of law, however significant, rarely receive such fame or adulation. The First Amendment is the rock star of the American Constitution. Its fame is justified, and this book seeks to offer some perspective on how special it is.

The Soul of the First Amendment

I

When the drafting of the United States Constitution was completed in Philadelphia early in September 1787, James Madison was pleased. The Articles of Confederation agreed upon by the states at the time of the Revolution had created an alliance of entities freed from British rule but not a functioning national government. The Framers of the Constitution, led by Madison, did that. In doing so, they made no effort to match the grace or passion of Thomas Jefferson's glowing revolutionary rhetoric in the Declaration of Independence of the previous decade. No inalienable rights were referred to in the new document, no paeans to human rights offered. The Constitution's language, as the historian Clinton Rossiter observed, was "plain to the point of severity, frugal to the point of austerity, laconic to the point of aphorism." It was not a prose-poem but a blueprint, one devoted to establishing a newly re-created and empowered government and setting forth how it would work. And it had been agreed upon after what John Adams characterized as "the greatest single effort of national deliberation that the world has ever seen." Madison's satisfaction at the result is reflected in a letter he wrote to Jefferson, his friend and mentor, then the American ambassador to France, which observed that "it is impossible to consider the degree of concord which ultimately prevailed as less than a miracle."

One topic on which there had been nearly complete concord was this: there would be no bill of rights in the Constitution. When a vote was taken on the subject, ten states voted against it; not one voted for it. The record of the Constitutional Convention summarizes the vote starkly: "On the question for a committee to prepare a Bill of Rights: New Hampshire no. Massachusetts, absent. Connecticut, no. New Jersey, no. Pennsylvania, no. Delaware, no. Maryland, no. Virginia, no. North Carolina, no. South Carolina, no. Georgia, no."

When two delegates, after the vote, sought a declaration stating "that the liberty of the press shall be inviolably observed," Roger Sherman responded that since "the power of the Congress does not extend to the press," it was unnecessary to specify that the press was protected against the government. By a seven-to-four vote, the Convention rejected the motion.

What may have seemed obvious enough to the delegates was far less so to others. Jefferson himself was appalled that the newly empowered national government would not be explicitly limited in its authority by specific prescriptions. It "astonishes me," Jefferson wrote, that "our countrymen . . . should be contented to live under a system which leaves to their governors the power of taking from them the trial by jury in civil cases, freedom of religion, freedom of the press," and other rights. "A bill of rights," he wrote to Madison, "is what the people are entitled to against every government on earth, general or particular, and what no just government should refuse, or rest on inference." Another Jeffersonian missive stated that he had "disapproved from the first moment . . . the want of a bill of rights to guard liberty against the legislative as well as the executive branches of the government."

Critics of the newly drafted Constitution were alarmed at the absence of a bill of rights. Patrick Henry, who opposed ratification of the Constitution before the Virginia legislature, observed that "a Bill of Rights may be summed up in a few words." If they are not used, Henry warned, "the officers of Congress may come upon you, fortified with all the terrors of paramount federal authority." In South Carolina, James Lincoln complained that he "would be glad to know why, in this Constitution, there is a total silence with respect to the liberty of the press. Was it forgotten? Impossible! Then it must have been purposely omitted; and with what design, good or bad, he left the world to judge. The liberty of the press was the tyrant's scourge—it was the true friend and firmest supporter of civil liberty; therefore why pass it by in silence?" In New York, *Cincinnatus*, one of a number of anonymous critics of the newly drafted Constitution, argued that "not only [is] some power . . . given in the constitution to restrain, and even to subject the press," but that the power to do so was "totally unlimited; and may certainly annihilate the freedom of the press, and convert it from being the palladium of liberty to become an engine of imposition and tyranny. It is an easy step from restraining the press to making it place the worst actions of government in so favorable a light, that we may groan under tyranny and oppression without knowing from whence it comes."

Responses from opponents of including a bill of rights in the Constitution offered views similar to those uttered by Sherman during the Constitutional Convention itself. Why, Alexander Hamilton responded, in much-quoted questions he posed in Federalist, No. 84, should the charter of the newly reorganized government "declare that things shall not be done which there is no power to do? Why for instance, should it be said, that the liberty of the press should not be restrained, when no power is given by which restrictions may be imposed?" In fact, Hamilton argued, "the constitution is itself in every rational sense, and to every useful purpose, A BILL OF RIGHTS."

Other opponents of adding a bill of rights offered similar views. Where, Virginia Governor Randolph asked, "is the page" in the Constitution "where [freedom of the press] is restrained? If there had been any regulation about it, leaving it insecure, then there might have been reason for clamors. But this is not the case. If it be, I again ask for the particular clause which gives liberty to destroy the freedom of the press." Others mocked the very notion of a bill of rights. "No bill of rights," Roger Sherman observed, "ever yet bound the supreme power longer than the honey moon of a newly married couple." And why, John Dickinson asked, was a bill of rights needed? "Do we want to be reminded, that the sun enlightens, warms, invigorates, and cheers? or how horrid it would be, to have his blessed beams intercepted, by our being thrust into mines or dungeons?" Noah Webster, tongue deeply in cheek, suggested that if a list of inalienable rights were to be added to the Constitution, it should include a clause stating that "every body shall, in good weather, hunt on his own land, and catch fish in rivers that are public property . . . [and] that Congress shall never restrain any inhabitant of America from eating and drinking, at seasonable times, or prevent his lying on his left side, in a long winter's night."

Madison had initially opposed the inclusion of a bill of rights, disparaging any such document as a useless "parchment barrie[r]" which "will never be regarded when opposed to the decided sense of the public." By the time Congress met in 1789, however, he had changed his strategy, if not his views. On a personal level, he had been shocked almost to have been defeated for reelection to the House by James Monroe, his later successor as president, who had actively supported the adoption of a bill of rights. At the same time, opponents of ratification of the Constitution were using the absence of a bill of rights as a basis for rejecting it and seemed likely to be preparing crippling amendments of their own that might make ratification significantly less likely. It would be better, he wrote to a friend, that amendments would "appear to be the free gift of the friends of the Constitution" rather than having been "extorted" from them by its enemies. Madison responded by shifting his position from opponent to draftsman, preparing the first draft of the document and introducing it to the House of Representatives of the First Congress with the tepid assertion that, given public concern about its absence, its inclusion offered "something to gain, and, if we proceed with caution, nothing to lose." As initially proposed on June 8, 1789, the equivalent of what became the First Amendment's language about freedom of speech and press reads generally similarly to what was finally adopted.

Except in one significant respect, Madison's first proposal on freedom of expression, submitted to the House, was phrased this way: "The people shall not be deprived or abridged of their right to speak, to write, or to publish their sentiments; and the freedom of the press, as one of the great bulwarks of liberty, shall be inviolable." By the time, on September 25, that the Senate had weighed in and the two Houses had agreed on language, what became the First Amendment was phrased in a manner that was couched not as affirmatively assuring the people of their rights but, in indelibly negative language, as assuring that Congress could not strip the public of those rights. The words *"Congress shall make no law"* were chosen to introduce the First Amendment, a decision that would lead the Supreme Court throughout American history to rule that the First Amendment barred only governmental, not private, suppression of speech.

What is most striking today when reading the debates over the adoption of a bill of rights is that while there was fiery disagreement about whether to adopt such a document at all, little of it appears to have been about what those rights were. Instead, the debates focused almost exclusively on whether it was necessary or even useful to add to the Constitution as it had been drafted in Philadelphia, either in its text or separately as amendments, any list of prohibited government actions at all. In the end, those who believed that without a bill of rights the newly empowered federal government might well overstep its bounds into areas of personal liberty carried the day, and what would eventually be viewed, as historian Joseph Ellis put it, as the nation's "secular version of the Ten Commandments" became binding law.

Inevitably, the language chosen for the Bill of Rights has been subject to multiple, sometimes conflicting interpretations. In addition, the passage of time has led to disputes about topics that would have been inconceivable in the eighteenth century. Who, for example, can speak with confidence today about what the Framers would have thought about net neutrality, videogames, or algorithms?

One view of the Framers, however, could hardly be clearer. The "great object" of bills of rights, Madison observed when he first introduced the Bill of Rights in the

House of Representatives, was "to limit and qualify the powers of Government, by excepting out of the grant of power those cases in which the Government ought not to act, or to act only in a particular mode." "Courts of justice," Madison optimistically predicted, would serve as "impenetrable barriers" to violations. Later, in the debates over the adoption of the Bill of Rights, Madison went further. With its adoption, he said, "the right of freedom of speech is secured; the liberty of the press is expressly declared to be beyond the reach of this Government." The imposition of strict limits on governmental authority over religion, speech, and press was the central purpose of the First Amendment. It is what the First Amendment is about.

That theme has been repeated by jurists with the widest divergence of views on other matters. Supreme Court Justice Robert H. Jackson, writing in 1945, put it this way: "The very purpose of the First Amendment is to foreclose public authority from assuming a guardianship of the public mind through regulating the press, speech, and religion. In this field, every person must be his own watchman for truth, because the forefathers did not trust any government to separate the true from the false for us." Justice Hugo Black, writing in 1961, observed that "the very reason for the First Amendment is to make the people of the country free to think, speak, write and worship as they wish, not as the Government commands." Justice William O. Douglas, in 1973, stated that "the struggle for liberty has been a struggle against Government. The essential scheme of our Constitution and Bill of Rights was to take Government off the backs of people." Justice John Paul Stevens observed in 1985 that "the First Amendment was adopted to curtail Congress' power to interfere with the individual's freedom to believe, to worship, and to express himself in accordance with the dictates of his own conscience." Justice Anthony Kennedy wrote in 2002 that "First Amendment freedoms are most in danger when the government seeks to control thought or to justify its laws for that impermissible end. The right to think is the beginning of freedom, and speech must be protected from the government because speech is the beginning of thought." Chief Justice John Roberts, in 2010, stated that "the First Amendment protects against the Government; it does not leave us at the mercy of *noblesse oblige*. We would not uphold an unconstitutional statute merely because the Government promised to use it responsibly."

So clearly established is the notion that the Bill of Rights in general and the First Amendment in particular exist to protect against the government that it would be easy to fill pages with similar quotations. But in recent years, that very notion has come under increasing attack from liberal critics of expansive First Amendment rulings of the Roberts Court. There is historical irony in this. It was not many years ago that it could fairly be said, in the words of University of Delaware political scientist Wayne Batchis, that "contemporary liberalism seemed to consistently stand on the side of the First Amendment, even when the short-term costs were perceived to be relatively high," while "political and jurisprudential conservatives, in contrast, saw a First Amendment that was less of an absolute—a guarantee that could be balanced more comfortably against the democratic needs of civility and morality in some areas or evaded entirely in others." Indeed, for most of American history, the First Amendment has generally served as what Yale Law School professor Jack Balkin has referred to as "the friend of left-wing values, whether it was French émigrés and Republicans in the 1790s, abolitionists in the 1840s, pacifists in the 1910s, organized labor in the 1920s and 1930s, or civil rights protesters in the 1950s and 1960s." In all these instances, as well as in more recent ones in which efforts were made to enjoin the press, to censor books, and to limit political expression by deeming criminal the burning of the American flag, opposition to broad First Amendment protections tended to come from the right.

Times have changed, however, and so have the issues raised before the Supreme Court dealing with freedom of expression. In some cases involving particularly obnoxious speech—the filming of animals being tortured and killed, for example, or vile demonstrations denouncing dead American soldiers on the days of their funerals—the Court has been all but unanimous in protecting loathsome speech to a degree that would be unimaginable elsewhere in the world. In an increasing number of cases, however, ranging from ones involving the rights of those who oppose abortions to have their say close to abortion clinics, to individuals who refrain from joining public employee unions and maintain that they should not be obliged to pay any dues to them, to individuals and companies who object to limits on their independent expenditures supporting candidates for public office, and to companies that engage in commercial speech, it has been the more conservative members of the Court who have been championing more expansive First Amendment protections. In those cases, more liberal jurists have not only differed with their conservative colleagues about the scope of the First Amendment but often taken positions that could more generally limit its impact.

A stark example is the Supreme Court's ruling in 2000 in a case involving a Colorado statute that made it criminal for anyone within one hundred feet of a health-care facility—that is to say, a facility in which abortions occurred—to "knowingly approach" another person within eight feet, without her consent, to engage in "oral protest, education, or counseling." As correctly summarized by the American Civil Liberties Union, in its amicus curiae brief supporting a First Amendment challenge to the law, it thus made criminal "advocacy . . . that does not threaten to impede or obstruct persons entering or leaving the clinic, including the simple act of handing out a leaflet." For many years before, the Court had repeatedly held that even speech viewed as offensive was protected by the First Amendment and that "our own citizens must tolerate insulting, and even outrageous, speech in order to provide adequate breathing space to the freedoms protected by the First Amendment."

In this case, *Hill v. Colorado*, the Court, in a six-to-three opinion of Justice Stevens, sought to elude these opinions by affirming the Colorado law's constitutionality based on what the Court characterized as the "privacy interest in avoiding unwanted communication," an interest it treated as an aspect of what Justice Louis Brandeis had long before called, in the very different context of government conduct, as the "right to be let alone." As Justice Antonin Scalia's dissenting opinion (joined by Justice Clarence

Thomas) demonstrated, Colorado had made no such argument in support of sustaining the statute. Indeed, it had explicitly rejected any attribution to it of such a basis for sustaining the law as a "straw interest," one not made by the state and one that it had repudiated. The strategic reason Colorado had done so was clear enough: only three years before, the Court declined to rely on that very contention as a basis for sustaining such a law and, in the course of doing so, had expressed "doubt" that this "right ... accurately reflects our First Amendment jurisprudence." Yet based primarily on that theory, a statute that criminalized the sort of speech the First Amendment most obviously generally protects—protests, education, and counseling on public property—was held constitutional. That was the ruling with respect to a statute that banned the speech regardless of whether it was at all threatening or whether the speaker had interfered in any way with access to the clinic. From any previously articulated First Amendment perspective, the ruling was insupportable, yet only three conservative members of the Court dissented.

Justice Kennedy's summary statement of the case in his dissent put it this way: "For the first time, the Court approves a law which bars a private citizen from passing a message, in a peaceful manner and on a profound moral issue, to a fellow citizen on a public sidewalk." His conclusion was memorable:

> Here the citizens who claim First Amendment protection seek it for speech which, if it is to be effective, must take place at the very time and place a grievous moral wrong, in their view, is about to occur. The Court tears away from the protesters the guarantees of the First Amendment when they most need it. So committed is the Court to its course that it denies these protesters, in the face of what they consider to be one of life's gravest moral crises, even the opportunity to try to offer a fellow citizen a little pamphlet, a handheld paper seeking to reach a higher law.

In 2014, *Hill* was effectively reversed by a unanimous vote of the Court in *McCullen v. Coakley,* a case that held that a Massachusetts law, similar in almost all respects to the one that the Court had held constitutional fourteen years before, was overbroad and thus unconstitutional. Not a word was said in the opinion for the Court, written by Chief Justice Roberts, about the Court's earlier reliance on any supposed right to be let alone. In fact, the ruling in *Hill* was so studiously ignored by the majority in all respects that Justice Scalia, in a concurring opinion in the case for himself, Justice Kennedy, and Justice Thomas, all but shouted that the effect of the new opinion was that *Hill* had been reversed. What remains of it, however, is a disturbing memory of how far the more liberal members of the Court had been prepared to go to sustain the constitutionality of a law that could not withstand the slightest First Amendment scrutiny. Justice Scalia attributed *Hill* to what he viewed as the pro-abortion views of the liberal jurists on the court. Whatever the motivation of the jurists in *Hill*'s majority, the Colorado statute at issue was, as Harvard Law School luminary Laurence Tribe put it, a "slam dunk" violation of the First Amendment. It should not have taken fourteen years to reject it.

Nor have the more liberal jurists on the Court limited their resistance to broad First Amendment protection for speech to cases such as *Hill*. In his book *Active Liberty: Interpreting Our Democratic Constitution*, Justice Stephen Breyer maintained that the primary purpose of the First Amendment "goes beyond" protecting the individual from government restrictions. "First and foremost," Breyer wrote, the First Amendment "seeks to facilitate democratic self-government." Correctly viewed, he maintained, one must "understand the First Amendment as seeking primarily to encourage the exchange of information and ideas necessary for citizens themselves to shape that 'public opinion which is the final source of government in a democratic state.'" In his dissenting opinion in the *McCutcheon v. Federal Election Commission* case, relating to limitations on the total amount of contributions a donor may make to candidates for Congress, in which he was joined by Justices Ruth Bader Ginsburg, Sonia Sotomayor, and Elena Kagan, Breyer argued similarly. "The First Amendment," he wrote, "advances not only the individual's right to engage in political speech, but also the public's interest in preserving a democratic order in which collective speech *matters.*" The First Amendment, he urged, must be understood as promoting a "government where laws reflect the very thoughts, views, ideas, and sentiments, the expression of which the First Amendment protects."

These views offer a double-barreled First Amendment, one that addresses not only the risks of governmental control over speech but the desirability of a government truly responsive to the views of the public. But there is reason to doubt that the First Amendment can serve both ends.

"First and foremost," after all, the First Amendment seeks to protect against the dangers of government overreaching into areas where government itself is especially dangerous—freedom of religion, speech, and press. At its core, it is not about promoting "collective speech" but of avoiding the imposition of just such speech by the government. One of the benefits of the First Amendment is that it generally leads to a better-informed public and ultimately a more representative government. But we surely would not allow particular speech to be suppressed because the government decided that it led the public to become ill-informed or less enamored of representative government. That sort of censorship is the opposite of what the First Amendment is about.

The notion that First Amendment interests are served whenever laws genuinely reflect public opinion also seems to overlook the reality that the public too often seeks to suppress speech it disapproves of. Speech is sometimes ugly, outrageous, even dangerous. The understandable public response to such speech is often one of disgust, revulsion, and sometimes anger. And support for taking steps to assure that the offending speech does not recur.

Who would doubt that the "collective speech" of the public would likely result in the banning of virtual child pornography on the Internet—lifelike depictions of children that, as a federal statute provided, "appear to be" engaged in sexual conduct, a statute held unconstitutional under the First Amendment in the *Ashcroft v. Free Speech Coalition* case in 2002 because the films at issue showed no real children at all but only virtual ones? Or that there were and are substantial majorities of the public that supported and would still support legislation held unconstitutional by the Supreme Court that banned the burning of the American flag? Or that the public, inconsistently with the First Amendment as interpreted by the Supreme Court, would overwhelmingly support punishing or at least silencing members of the Westboro Baptist Church, whose contemptible practice is to coarsely denounce American soldiers who have died in the service of their country on the days of their funerals in sites as close to the churches where those funerals are held as the police will allow?

Chief Justice Roberts's pungent response to the Breyer opinion in *McCutcheon v. Federal Election Commission* is cogent: "The dissent's 'collective speech' . . . is of course the will of the majority, and plainly can include laws that restrict free speech. The whole point of the First Amendment is to afford individuals protection against such infringements. The First Amendment does not protect the government, even when the government purports to act through legislation reflecting 'collective speech.'"

A consistent supporter of the Breyer view of the First Amendment is the Brennan Center, a liberal think-tank named after one of the Supreme Court's greatest and most consistent defenders of the First Amendment. In a 2016 paper, the center approvingly quotes from the line in the Breyer dissent that concludes by referring to "the public's interest in preserving a democratic order in which collective speech *matters*" and by offering its view that "massive contributions weaken the link between public opinion and political action by making public opinion harder to hear. Recognizing that the Constitution protects the public's ability as a whole to make their views known could reverse the last decade of Supreme Court jurisprudence."

The Brennan Center's argument about how to make public opinion *easier* to hear and better known amounts to nothing less than limiting the speech of those it seems to believe talk too much. Justice Brennan himself disagreed with that approach, joining the 1976 *Buckley v. Valeo* ruling of the Court, which reached precisely the opposite conclusion that "the concept that government may restrict the speech of some elements of our society in order to enhance the relative voice of others is wholly foreign to the First Amendment."

No theoretical justification for protecting free expression provides any basis for ignoring the pervasive skepticism reflected in the First Amendment of governmental limits on or punishment of speech. Thomas Emerson, the patriarch of First Amendment scholars, has asserted as the first premise of what he characterized as the "system of freedom of expression" the proposition that the First Amendment serves the interest of "assuring individual self-fulfillment"—which can only be achieved when one's mind is free. Others have emphasized the benefits of freedom of expression in assuring that the public has all information necessary to determine what is true, the desirability of the public hearing the widest array of views to enable it to pass on issues of public policy, and the necessity of the public being trained by exposure to the widest range of views in the need for tolerance of those with whom they may differ. The core teaching of the First Amendment is that those values are served best by limiting the power of government over speech, not augmenting it.

Of course, the First Amendment is obviously not the only liberty-protecting provision of the Bill of Rights. If it were, we would not need the other nine amendments of the original Bill of Rights or the post–Civil War amendments that ended slavery, required states to provide due process of law, and effectively subjected state governments to most of the same limitations on liberty that were initially applied only to the federal government. Unreasonable searches and seizures by federal and state governments are banned; trials in both federal and state courts must be fair; cruel and unusual punishments are barred in both. What all of these limitations have in common is not that they are all about speech but they are all about limiting potential governmental abuse of power.

So when Burt Neuborne, in his book *Madison's Music*, disapproves of recent broad First Amendment rulings protecting speech by asking, "What should frighten us more? A democratically elected government tweaking the speech market to protect the weak or a wholly unregulated speech market dominated by a few massive corporations?," he simply ignores the thrust of the Bill of Rights as a whole, and the First Amendment in particular, which are all about limiting the power of our "democratically elected government."

That does not mean that limitations may not be placed on the size or behavior of private entities, including corporations. Antitrust and many other laws limit their behavior and could, if Congress chooses, be stronger still. But only the government has police and prisons. Only the government can impose fines. And only the government can treat as criminal the televising of a documentary close to primaries or elections that denounces a leading candidate for the presidency. That is what the *Citizens United* case was about. Whatever else one may conclude about that case, it hardly involved some sort of mere "tweak" of the "speech market."

Another example of disparagement of recent First Amendment rulings was a 2015 article by Lincoln Caplan, who has written many pieces for the *New York Times* editorial board and elsewhere about the First Amendment. In an article in the *American Scholar* entitled "The Embattled First Amendment," he wrote:

However sacred the idea of free speech remains for us today, we should recognize that its most fervent champions are not standing up for mistrusted outliers . . . or for the dispossessed and powerless. Today's advocates do the bidding of insiders—the super-rich and the ultra-powerful, the airline, drug, petroleum, and tobacco industries, all the winners in America's winner-take-all society. In a country where the gap between the haves and have-nots has grown so extreme that both political parties now pay lip service to populism, the haves have seized free speech as their cause—and their shield.

Tim Wu, a Columbia University law professor, offered similar views in an article on corporations and the First Amendment in the *New Republic* magazine entitled "The Right to Evade Regulation." He expressed his concern that "the mighty, as well as the marginalized," were asserting the First Amendment as a defense in a wide variety of cases. Once "the patron saint of protesters and the disenfranchised," Wu wrote, "the First Amendment has become the darling of economic libertarians and corporate lawyers who have recognized its power to immunize private enterprise from legal restraint."

Both Caplan and Wu raise serious issues about how the First Amendment should be interpreted. But their focus on the identity of those asserting First Amendment claims, as if that should determine or even affect the scope of constitutional protection, is disturbing. Many of the most memorable First Amendment cases have indeed afforded broad protection to "mistrusted outsiders" and the "marginalized." A vigilantly enforced First Amendment often does so by assuring that unpopular views may be voiced by those who would significantly, even radically, change aspects of American society. But just as the Fourth Amendment's bar of unreasonable searches and seizures protects everyone, whether the victim is an individual or Google, the First Amendment protects the speech of all, without regard to whether they are insiders or outsiders, economic libertarians or socialists. A First Amendment that was applied based upon the economic or social status of those claiming its protections, whatever they may be, would be politicized, one-sided, and ultimately lacking in legitimacy.

Kathleen Sullivan, the former dean of the Stanford Law School, writing in the *Harvard Law Review*, addressed the same issue, observing that there are currently "two very different visions of free speech" in conflict. One "conceives of speech rights as protected to the extent that they serve the end of political equality, and regulable to the extent that political equality cuts the other way." The other is rooted in the quite different concept that the "core concern" of the First Amendment "is negative rather than affirmative—to restrain government from 'abridging. . .

speech' rather than to protect 'rights' that require the antecedent step of identifying appropriate rights holders."

She is undoubtedly correct that there are two such views of the First Amendment, but only the "liberty" view appears consistent with the text or purport of it. To conclude that the First Amendment should *not* fully protect the political liberties of all but only those viewed as disenfranchised would not only be inconsistent with the core concern of the First Amendment of avoiding governmental control over speech but could ultimately threaten the liberties of us all. Censorship is contagious. Permitting the government—the very entity the First Amendment was adopted to protect against—to limit the speech of some inevitably would risk the rights of all.

What sort of speech is encompassed within the phrase "the freedom of speech and of the press"? How and to what extent shall First Amendment interests be protected when other deeply rooted (and sometimes constitutionally rooted) interests are also at stake? Some speech—spying, for example, or perjury—has simply been held to be not the sort of "speech" the First Amendment has ever been thought to protect. Other speech—libel and obscenity, for instance—have historically been subjected to sanctions and still are, but in a manner that accommodates First Amendment concerns by limiting the scope of both bodies of law. Other speech—involving reporting by the press of potentially prejudicial materials about defendants about to be tried—has led the Supreme Court in the *Nebraska Press Association* case to conclude that since prior restraints on reporting "are the most serious and the least tolerable infringement on First Amendment rights," that even when a defendant's right to fair trial is at risk, no such restraint may issue in the absence of proof that no other means could assure a fair trial, that "further publicity, unchecked, would so distort the views of potential jurors that 12 could not be found" who would follow the Court's instructions, and that in fact the entry of a prior restraint would assure such a result. Given such sweeping limitations on the entry of such orders, they are now all but unknown in American jurisprudence. As for speech which is alleged to threaten national security, criminal sanctions and even prior restraints may be available to prevent great harm to the nation, but only in the rarest circumstance as to each. As a result, the almost farcically overbroad Espionage Act of 1917 has been read narrowly when speech was involved and prior restraints have been held available (as Justice Potter Stewart concluded in his decisive concurring opinion in the Pentagon Papers case) only when publication would "surely result in direct, immediate, and irreparable harm" to the nation.

It is no surprise that the case-by-case development of First Amendment law has sometimes seemed confusing. The difficulty of interpretation is compounded by the reality that for all its eighteenth-century lineage, the First Amendment was not seriously explored and then applied in opinions of the Supreme Court until well into the twentieth century.

At the beginning of that century, First Amendment protections were decidedly frail. I had occasion, early in this century, to prepare an introduction to a book called *Political Censorship* containing *New York Times* articles on censorship published from 1900 through 1999. Doing so from a twenty-first-century First Amendment perspective was startling. Until well into the twentieth century, censorship was rampant. It was as if the First Amendment had yet to be written. A number of the *Times*'s articles, published in the first decade of the twentieth century, are illustrative. All reported on censorial acts, not one of which was viewed as a First Amendment violation at the time. Not one would be constitutionally permissible today.

For example, a 1901 dispatch matter-of-factly reports on the sentencing to jail of the managing editor and a reporter of the *Chicago American* for publishing an article critical "of the court's decision on an application for the forfeiture of the charter of the People's Gaslight and Coke

Company." According to the judge who sentenced them, "if the matter published were allowed to go unnoticed by the court it paved the way for other attacks, and that the judiciary, if not held, in respect, would fall, with all democratic government."

Five years later, an article described the indictment of three Saint Paul newspapers for reporting on the hanging of a criminal, on the basis of a law that forbade "publication of details of a hanging." Under the law, the *Times* reported, "newspapers are permitted simply to announce the fact of the execution." The expected punishment for reporting otherwise was a fine.

Three years after that, Spokane authorities were reported to have seized "every copy" of the *Industrial Worker,* the house organ of the Industrial Workers of the World, for reporting about the "alleged experience" of a prisoner in the county jail. According to the city, the article was libelous. "The papers," the *Times* reported without comment, "will be burned."

In the same decade, direct censorship of the arts was the norm. In 1901, the *Times* reported that commissioners of the District of Columbia had adopted regulations "designed to prohibit theatrical performances which are offensive to decency." Police, the paper duly reported, "are the censors, and are to decide what shows are immoral, though, of course, the final decision rests with the courts." Included in the law was a "provision which a zealous police officer might interpret as prohibiting burlesque or comic opera costumes."

On-the-ground police censorship in New York City of stage presentations involved the same boundless degree of authority to determine what might or might not be shown. One 1908 article described the arrest of a theatrical performer who had delivered, on a Sunday, a mock political speech in dialect. He was arrested, as an acting police captain put it, for the crime of impersonating a German. Another police intervention was described as having been taken pursuant to a police-created policy of permitting "acting" while banning "vaudeville." The *Times* duly, and with an apparent straight face, reported the police watching a quartet sing and then seeing "between two of the songs, the baritone [striking] the second tenor with a newspaper." "Cut that out," the policeman yelled, "that's vaudeville."

Cultural censorship was routine. A 1916 article described a Pennsylvania law banning films "showing safe-crackers at work, tramps stealing watches, and people taking drugs." So were many "thrillers, with heroines tied to tracks." A striking example of direct cultural censorship was offered in a 1921 article under the headline "Improper Novel Costs Women $100." The article began:

> Margaret C. Anderson and Jane Heap, publisher and editor respectively of The Little Review, at 27 West Eighth Street, each paid a fine of $50 imposed by Justices McInerney, Kernochan and Moss in Special Sessions yesterday, for publishing an improper novel in the July and August, 1920, issues of the magazine. John S. Summer, Secretary of the New York Society for the Prevention of Vice, was the complainant. The defendants were accompanied to court by several Greenwich Village artists and writers.
>
> John Quinn, counsel for the women, told the court that the alleged objectionable story, entitled "Ulysses," was the product of one Joyce, author, playwright and graduate of Dublin University, whose work had been praised by noted critics. "I think that this novel is unintelligible," said Justice McInerney.

The final line of the article stated that "the court held that parts of the story seemed to be harmful to the morals of the community." Accordingly, the book was suppressed. Not for another dozen years was Joyce's masterpiece permitted into the country.

And not until a series of enduring opinions of Justices Oliver Wendell Holmes and Louis Brandeis, often in dissent, commencing in the 1920s, did serious juridical exploration of the First Amendment even begin; not until 1925 was the First Amendment held applicable to the states; and not until 1965 was a federal statute held to be unconstitutional under the First Amendment.

When twentieth-century jurists looked at the eighteenth-century First Amendment, they were confronted anew with the so deliberately negatively phrased Bill of Rights. Why phrase the amendments in such a negative fashion by focusing on what Congress (and, later, other governmental actors) may *not* do? Why focus on barring the government from abridging rights rather than simply asserting that the public retained them?

Norman Cousins, the editor more than half a century ago of the *Saturday Review of Literature*, put it this way: "The principal values of democracy are negative. Those restraints operate primarily upon government itself. There is the logical belief that power is a natural invitation to tyranny, and that therefore the only safe repository of ultimate power is in the people themselves. . . . The one word most expressive of democracy is 'no.' Democracy says 'no' to the government that would invade the natural rights of the individual or the group. . . . This is not to say that democracy lacks affirmative values. The affirmative values are many and varied, but they all rest on a solid bedrock of restraints upon government."

II

Suppose the views of those who attended the Constitutional Convention in 1787 that no bill of rights was needed or advisable had carried the day. What sorts of expression would have been lost?

One way to tell is by looking at cases in which government limitations on speech have been held to violate the First Amendment. For example: if there had been no First Amendment in effect in 1943, a child whose religion forbade her from saluting the American flag could have been expelled from her public school for "insubordination" until she did so. If there had been no First Amendment in effect in 1964, southern white juries would have been free to continue down the path of imposing staggering and company-threatening libel verdicts against national publications such as the *New York Times* as they reported on the civil rights revolution. If there had been no First Amendment in effect in 1974, theaters that showed the movie *Carnal Knowledge* could have been successfully prosecuted for violating obscenity laws. More recently, only the existence of the First Amendment has protected controversial and what some find to be disturbing expression ranging from the burning of an American flag as a form of protest, demonstrations close to facilities offering abortions, and the spending of unlimited sums by individuals and corporations in support of or in opposition to candidates for public office.

Consider another counterfactual alternative. Suppose the Bill of Rights as a whole and the First Amendment in particular had been phrased differently. Suppose, instead of stating in unambiguously negative terms that Congress could not abridge freedom of speech or press, the First Amendment had been phrased affirmatively. What if it had been written this way: "Every person shall have the right to freedom of thought, conscience, and belief. Every person shall have the freedom of speech and expression, which include the freedom of the press and other media." Or, more simply, this way: "Citizens are guaranteed freedom of speech, of the press, of assembly, demonstration, and association."

We know that Madison would have been delighted to have included a reference to freedom of conscience in the Bill of Rights. He fought hard and unsuccessfully to have just that concept included. As for saying that "every person" or "citizen" was entitled to protection of freedom of expression, if any such language had been adopted as the First Amendment, it might well have been interpreted by the Supreme Court to have barred not just the government but private entities—Google and Facebook, for example—from limiting freedom of expression. That First Amendment might well have been read to oblige the government not only to avoid abridging freedom of speech, free press, and the like by its own conduct but to protect it against all comers.

But we should not too easily be misled into thinking that the language of a constitutional provision will necessarily guarantee its realization in practice. The first articulation above is from article 19 of the constitution of Eritrea, the second from article 67 of the constitution of North Korea. They rank, in a recent assessment by Reporters Without Borders, as the two most brutally repressive states in the world, with neither permitting any expression of views inconsistent with that of their governments and both rooted in the notion that all media outlets are nothing but government mouthpieces. The freedom-protective language in their constitutions are empty conceits, see-through camouflage of nations that are rooted neither in any concept of law nor in that of individual liberty.

That is not the case of democratic nations around the world, even if they do not share the American view of First Amendment transcendence. In Canada, for example, when William Whatcott, a religious zealot, was outraged that high schools in Saskatchewan were about to teach about homosexuality, he placed flyers in mailboxes stating that "if Saskatchewan's sodomites have their way, your school board will be celebrating buggery too," and that the teaching would amount to telling "children . . . how wonderful it is for two men to sodomize each other." His speech was held to be criminal, in violation of a statute that prohibits expression that "ridicules, belittles or otherwise affronts the dignity of any person or class of persons" on the basis of a prohibited ground.

When the Canadian equivalent of the First Amendment was raised as a defense, the Supreme Court of Canada affirmed the conviction. Its basis for doing so was thoughtful, sensitive, and powerful. It was also flatly at odds with long-standing American jurisprudence. Here is the way the

Canadian Supreme Court expressed the justification for treating as criminal Whatcott's hate-filled flyers:

> Hate speech is an effort to marginalize individuals based on their membership in a group. Using expression that exposes the group to hatred, hate speech seeks to delegitimize group members in the eyes of the majority, reducing their social standing and acceptance within society. Hate speech, therefore, rises beyond causing distress to individual group members. It can have a societal impact. Hate speech lays the groundwork for later, broad attacks on vulnerable groups that can range from discrimination, to ostracism, segregation, deportation, violence and, in the most extreme cases, to genocide. Hate speech also impacts on a protected group's ability to respond to the substantive ideas under debate, thereby placing a serious barrier to their full participation in our democracy.

The Court went on to assert that "the benefits of the suppression of hate speech and its harmful effects outweigh the detrimental effect of restricting expression which, by its nature, does little to promote the values underlying freedom of expression."

American law could hardly be more inconsistent. When a family of religious zealots that formed what it characterized as the Westboro Baptist Church carried signs a thousand feet from a church where the death of an American soldier in Afghanistan was being mourned, saying that his death was deserved because of American tolerance of gays, similarly bigoted language was held protected by the First Amendment. The signs screamed, "God Hates Fags," "Fags Doom Nations," "Fag Troops," and "Semper Fi Fags." The Supreme Court, in *Snyder v. Phelps*, concluded: "While these messages may fall short of refined social or political commentary, the issues they highlight—the political and moral conduct of the United States and its citizens, the fate of our Nation, homosexuality in the military, and scandals involving the Catholic clergy—are matters of public import. . . . [The] speech is 'fairly characterized as constituting speech on a matter of public concern.'"

The Court went further. Far from ruling that such speech provided a basis for punishment, it said that such speech was entitled to "special protection" under the First Amendment because of the public importance of the topics it had addressed. "Such speech," the Court emphasized, "cannot be restricted simply because it is upsetting or arouses contempt."

As for the view of the Canadian court that hate speech "does little to promote the values underlying freedom of expression," American courts might well respond that the ultimate First Amendment value is the avoidance of government censorship without regard to the worth of the speech itself. Confronted in 2010 with the issue of whether a statute that banned the filming of "crush videos" and other depictions of the torture and killing of animals was constitutional, Chief Justice Roberts denounced a balancing test proposed by the government that would have read as follows: "'Whether a given category of speech enjoys First Amendment protection depends upon a categorical balancing of the value of the speech against its societal costs.'"

In *United States v. Stevens*, the Court's dismissal of that test was merciless. The proposed test was "startling and dangerous." Why? Because the "First Amendment's guarantee of free speech does not extend only to categories of speech that survive an ad hoc balancing of relative social costs and benefits." Because "the First Amendment itself reflects a judgment by the American people that the benefits of its restrictions on the Government outweigh the costs." Because "our Constitution forecloses any attempt to revise that judgment simply on the basis that some speech is not worth it."

Throughout Europe, harsh and accusatory criticism of the alleged misbehavior of Muslim immigrants from Islamic nations and the supposedly baleful impact of their unassimilated presence throughout the continent has led to criminal prosecutions for speech, prosecutions that would be unthinkable and undoubtedly unconstitutional in the United States. In Belgium, a member of Parliament and leader of a right-wing political party was convicted in 2009 for distributing leaflets calling for a "Belgians and European *First*" policy and saying, "Stop the Sham Immigration Policy, Send non-European sub-seekers home," and "Stand up against the Islamification of Belgium." He was convicted of incitement to racial discrimination, disqualified from holding office for ten years, and sentenced to community service. His conviction was affirmed by the European Court of Human Rights on the ground that such literature "sought to make fun of the immigrants," leading to hatred of foreigners, particularly by "less knowledgeable members of the public."

In England an individual was tried and convicted for carrying a poster that showed the World Trade Center ablaze with the caption "Islam out of Britain—Protect the British People." The European Court of Human Rights let the conviction stand, concluding that since the poster constituted a "public expression of attack on all Muslims in the United Kingdom" the speech could provide a basis for criminal sanctions. In a later case, a speaker was convicted of violating the English Malicious Communications Act after posting statements deemed "grossly offensive" to

Muslims, including one stating, "Don't come over to this country and treat it like your own. Britain first."

An apt comparison is the American reaction to a spate of incendiary assertions by Donald Trump in the course of his campaign for the presidency, ranging from denunciations of Mexicans ("They're bringing drugs. They're bringing crime. They're rapists") to repeated proposals to bar all Muslims from entering the United States for an unspecified time period. There was much criticism of those incendiary and inherently racist statements. But it was never suggested that such language was or could have been deemed criminal in the United States, as it could well have been in many European nations.

A similar divergence of approaches exists with respect to verbal or written attacks on or mockery of religious beliefs. In Poland, for example, an article of its criminal code makes criminal "offense to religious feelings" as well as "public calumny." In 2010, a singer was convicted of giving "intentional offense to religious feelings" for saying that she "believed more in dinosaurs than the Bible" because "it is hard to believe in something written by people who drank too much wine and smoked herbal cigarettes." Three years earlier, a rock musician was accused of the same crime for calling the Catholic Church "the most murderous cult on the planet."

When the comedian Bill Maher says much the same thing on American television—he does so frequently—he is laughed at or disparaged, but not indicted.

How different is the American approach? The International Covenant on Civil and Political Rights, drafted in 1966 and thereafter ratified by most nations in the world, provides in article 20 that "any advocacy of national, racial or religious hatred that constitutes incitement to discrimination, hostility or violence shall be prohibited by law." But what is "incitement to discrimination"? Although the United States does recognize that even in the face of an extremely broadly written First Amendment, incitement to violent acts can in certain narrow circumstances be penalized, any notion of "incitement to discrimination" could be interpreted far more broadly than the First Amendment permits. As a result, when the United States ratified the covenant in 1992, it was with the express reservation that "article 20 does not authorize or require legislation or other action by the United States that would restrict the right of free speech and association protected by the Constitution . . . of the United States."

The classic American case on the subject, *Cantwell v. Connecticut*, began on a street corner in New Haven in 1938. On April 26, 1938, Newton Cantwell and his two sons, all of whom were Jehovah's Witnesses, arrived on a street in New Haven in a neighborhood in which 90 percent of the residents were Roman Catholic. The Cantwells were equipped with a record player and a bag containing books and pamphlets of their religion's preachings. They went door to door and with the answerer's permission played one of their records. The Cantwells stopped two passersby, both Catholics, and asked for and received their permission to play a record. What they heard, entitled "Enemies," was an angry, sometimes venomous, attack on organized religion in general and the Roman Catholic Church in particular. Among the passages contained on the record, and played for and to its listeners, was this one:

> The most seductive and subtle instrument employed to deceive man is religion, because religion has the appearance of doing good, whereas it brings upon the people great evil. There are many different religions, all of which are deceptive, are the instruments of the enemy Satan, and all work to the injury of men. This book submits the conclusive proof that for more than fifteen hundred years a great religious system, operating out of Rome, has by means of fraud and deception brought untold sorrow and suffering upon the people. It operates the greatest racket ever employed amongst men and robs the people of their money and destroys their peace of mind and freedom of action. That religious system is vigorously pushing in its political schemes amongst all the nations

of earth, with the avowed purpose of seizing control of the nations and ruling the people by cruel dictators. Some of the nations have fallen under that wicked power, and all nations are now greatly endangered. Because of the increasing power of the enemy the liberties of the people are rapidly passing away and all nations are rushing into infidelity and into ultimate destruction.

Upon hearing such assertions and others that referred to the Church as a "harlot" that brought fascism and Nazism into being, one of the listeners told the Cantwells that they had better leave the area before something happened to them. They did so, but were later convicted of, among other things, inciting breach of the peace. The US Supreme Court ultimately reversed the convictions, concluding that "the fundamental law declares the interest of the United States that the free exercise of religion be not prohibited and that freedom to communicate information and opinion be not abridged." While a state has a right to reserve peace and order within its borders, the Court said, it "may not unduly suppress free communication of views, religious or other, under the guise of conserving desirable conditions."

The Cantwells, the Court said, were on a public street, where they had every right to be and to impart their views peacefully to others. They had sought and received the permission of those they had met to play their record. They had not impeded traffic.

The essential characteristic of political and religious liberty, the Court concluded, was that people could express their views "unmolested and unobstructed." In a country like the United States where people from so many nations and creeds coexist, the Court said, the shield that protects the right to exercise and disseminate different religions was especially necessary. "In the realm of religious faith," the Court explained, as well as

> that of political belief, sharp differences arise. In both fields the tenets of one man may seem the rankest error to his neighbor. To persuade others to his own point of view, the pleader, as we know, at times, resorts to exaggeration, to vilification of men who have been, or are, prominent in church or state, and even to false statement. But the people of this nation have ordained in the light of history, that, in spite of the probability of excesses and abuses, these liberties are, in the long view, essential to enlightened opinion and right conduct on the part of the citizens of a democracy.

In some nations, limitations on speech arise directly from disturbing, even sickening, events of their past. Holocaust denial is criminal in a number of nations, including Germany. Given Germany's genocidal history, there is no need to explain why. As Professor Michel Rosenfeld of Benjamin N. Cardozo School of Law has written, "Viewed from the particular perspective of a rejection of the Nazi experience and an attempt to prevent its resurgence, the suppression of hate speech seems both obvious and commendable."

Similarly, in India, section 153A of the Indian Penal Code criminalizes speech "promoting enmity between different groups on grounds of religion, race, place of birth," and the like. Throughout India's history, the communal violence that such provisions were adopted to prevent has recurred during electoral campaigns after critical, sometimes damning, comments directed at religious groups. Thousands of people have perished as a result of violence sparked by such statements, often around the times elections have been held. As summarized in the *Harvard Law Review* by New York University School of Law professor Samuel Issacharoff:

> The question is what steps may be taken to permit genuine, even if distasteful, political expression while maintaining public order in the face of likely violent outbursts. . . .
>
> . . . India's response is to narrow the definition of permissible political speech. . . .
>
> . . . In the stable framework of the United States, it may well be that reactions to suppress political participation have been overwrought and largely unnecessary. . . .

The decision of India, a country forged in fratricidal religious conflict, seeking to suppress election day incitements likely to engender communal violence is not a move so readily discounted.

It is understandable that some nations have sometimes responded by limiting particularly hateful speech that may have contributed to past tragedies. The United States has been fortunate not to have suffered such horrific events, and I am unwilling to criticize nations that have responded to such calamities by urging them to change their policies. For this nation, though, strict constitutionally imposed limitations on such legislation have served us well.

By twenty-first-century American standards, libel law as it is enforced in England (and as it was once enforced in the United States) has significantly limited freedom of expression. In England, defamatory statements—statements holding a person up to ridicule or obloquy or which cause a reasonable person to think less of him or her—are presumed to be false and the party who has uttered them must affirmatively prove their truth in a libel action. A good-faith belief in what was said is no defense, whatever the power or prominence of the criticized party. English judges, as legal scholars and practitioners Geoffrey Robertson and Andrew Nicol have observed, have "constructed a vast libel industry on the illogical presumption that defamatory statements are false."

This, together with other pro-plaintiff rules and regulations, resulted in England becoming a sort of legal paradise for those who commenced libel actions, with a success rate of over 90 percent in such cases. A number of notorious cases through the years brought about unjust results, only determined to be so long after libel litigations had led to judgments for those who sued or substantial settlements. Liberace, for example, won a celebrated case against a gossip columnist who had suggested he was gay; he was. John Profumo, while the minister of war, won libel damages for the published assertion that he had become sexually involved with a prostitute; he had. So had the author Jeffrey Archer, who was awarded significant damages as a result of the publication of newspaper articles linking him with a prostitute; his false testimony was revealed only years after the trial and he was jailed. Lance Armstrong, flush with drug-aided victories in bicycle races around the world, obtained damages and settlements from English publications that, as it turned out, had truthfully referred to his use of a variety of those drugs; only years later did Armstrong acknowledge his lies.

A less dramatic example was made public more recently when it became known that Cambridge University Press had declined to publish a book prepared for it that accused Russian president Vladimir Putin of having extensive connections with gangster elements in his country. Cambridge declined to publish the book, stating that as a matter of "risk tolerance" it could not risk a libel suit. "We have no reason to doubt," it wrote the author, "the veracity of what you say," but the risk of litigation and in any event "the disruption and expense" of such a litigation "would be more than we could afford, given our charitable and academic mission." The book was not published in England. It was published in the United States, and no litigation followed.

The reason the book about Putin could be published in the United States with little concern for libel actions following is its different, far more speech-protective path. Beginning with the momentous decision of the Supreme Court in *New York Times Company v. Sullivan* in 1964, at least in cases commenced by public officials (and, later, public figures), the burden is placed on the party suing to prove the falsity of the charges. A plaintiff in such a case must do still more, proving by clear and convincing evidence that the false statement was made with actual knowledge of falsity or serious doubts as to its truth—"actual malice," in the infelicitous words chosen by the Supreme

Court to describe it. If the defamatory statement was believed, however wrongly, it cannot provide a basis for liability.

So great is the difference between English and American libel law that English libel judgments are generally no longer enforceable in the United States as a result of a statute unanimously passed by the United States Senate in 2010 and signed into law by President Barack Obama. The new law was adopted in response to a libel action filed in England by Khalid bin Mahfouz, a Saudi billionaire, who sued Rachel Ehrenfeld in England following allegations by her about alleged connections between him and his charities and the funding of terrorism. In her book, entitled *Funding Evil: How Terrorism Is Financed and How to Stop It*, Ehrenfeld, an American citizen, had relied, in making her charges, upon numerous sources, including statements made by the Federal Reserve Board, a report of a United States Senate committee, the Islamic Human Rights Commission, and various books and articles. None of them would have been admissible in the English proceeding commenced by bin Mahfouz.

Although only twenty-three copies of the book were sold in England, the case proceeded there. (Later adopted reforms to English libel law would likely no longer permit this.) Ehrenfeld refused to appear, and a judgment of $225,000 was entered against her. In the United States, Ehrenfeld would likely have prevailed since bin Mahfouz would in all likelihood have been held to be a public figure and been unable to meet the First Amendment–protective burdens imposed upon such people. In England, chances seemed slim at best, and Ehrenfeld did not, in any event, have personal funding of the sort that would have allowed her to defend herself.

In response to the English judgment awarded against Ehrenfeld, various states adopted legislation barring the enforcement in their courts of libel judgments obtained in foreign courts that have legal systems without free speech protections such as that provided by the First Amendment. Not long afterward, Congress passed a law, entitled the SPEECH Act, with similar limitations imposed throughout the nation. Since no foreign nations have such provisions—First Amendment protections in the United States in libel actions are unique—the ultimate result appears to be that virtually no foreign libel judgments are now enforceable in the United States.

Elsewhere in Europe, as a 2014 International Press Institute survey reveals, criminal punishments for defamation are available in twenty-three European Union nations, and imprisonment is a possible punishment in twenty of them. In some nations, defamation penalties are greater when the offending language is directed at public officials. A 2015 report of the Committee to Protect Journalists cites laws in Bulgaria, France, Germany, Italy, Portugal, and the Netherlands as examples. Such an approach could hardly be more inconsistent with the American view that freedom of expression is especially protected when criticism of government is involved, including "unpleasantly sharp attacks on government and public officials."

In other areas of law, as well, American law provides far more protection for free expression than that provided elsewhere. European privacy law, as James Q. Whitman has observed, focuses on protecting the "personal honor" of individuals, whereas American law protects, in this area as in so many others, what is at its core a liberty interest. As a result, continental law reflects a desire to protect the public face of individuals at the same time that American law "shows a far greater sensitivity to intrusions on the part of the state."

Two European cases illustrate the difference.

*

In Finland, a nation repeatedly ranked by Reporters Without Borders as the single most protective in the world in protecting freedom of speech and of the press, an autobiographical book was written by Susan Ruusunen, the former girlfriend of the Finnish prime minister. Published while he was in office, it contained, among other things, information about their affair (the prime minister was divorced at the time), including aspects of their sexual relationship. Charged criminally under Finnish law for disseminating information about the private life of the prime minister in a manner conducive to causing him suffering or contempt, she was convicted of that crime and fined. Her conviction was affirmed by the Finnish supreme court and, in 2014, by the European Court of Human Rights. Both courts agreed that the publication, however truthful, of "information and hints about their sex life and intimate events between her and the Prime Minister" violated his "right to private life."

One need not reach far for an apt American analogy, even if hypothetical in nature. Imagine if Monica Lewinsky had written a book about her involvement with President Bill Clinton and it had been published during his presidency. Put aside the national mockery of the president that would have followed the filing of any such action by him claiming some sort of breach of his privacy. What is plain as a legal matter is that any such litigation would have been dismissed on First Amendment grounds, in all likelihood in a memorably scathing opinion.

In Germany, Princess Caroline of Monaco commenced a number of privacy-rooted lawsuits against various magazines for publishing photographs of her, her husband, and her children in various public sites. In one of them, the European Court of Human Rights concluded that since she held no public office and the photos, which were not intimate or embarrassing, nonetheless did not relate to her official duties, an order should bar such intrusion into her private life. A later ruling, after the application of a detailed balancing test, rejected her request for additional relief. All the claims would likely have been summarily rejected in the United States.

All these examples illustrate the degree to which the United States is an outlier in protecting speech that other democratic nations, in the service of other serious values, limit, punish, or bar altogether. It is not that American law protects all speech of all people at all times. Libel law exists; plaintiffs still sue and sometimes prevail, notwithstanding the far more stringent barriers to their doing so in the United States than in any other nation. Privacy law, as well, permits recovery in some cases, although far less often than in Europe. The victory in 2016 of the professional wrestler Hulk Hogan in such an action against the blog Gawker for showing portions of a surreptitiously taped sexual engagement is an example.

On even more threatening turf, the ever-potentially restrictive American Espionage Act adopted during World War I remains on the books and is enforced. And some classes of people—prisoners, schoolchildren, members of the armed forces, other government employees, and foreign speakers, for example—receive significantly less protection for their speech than do others.

Nor is it the case that American law has invariably protected speech to a greater degree than in Europe. A ruling of the Norwegian Supreme Court in December 2015, for example, relating to unpublished film material seized by the police from a documentary filmmaker provides an extremely high level of protection for journalists seeking to protect their confidential sources, one that American journalists could only view with envy.

As in Europe before and after the American Revolution, US history is filled with deeply troubling examples of free speech crumbling in times of crisis in the face of legislation and governmental pressure. Shortly after ratification of the Constitution, the Sedition Act of 1798 was adopted, making criminal a good deal of criticism of the president and other high-ranking officials. That repressive law, adopted by the John Adams administration, led to the jailing of more than twenty newspaper editors and was the single greatest frontal attack on freedom of speech in the nation's history. Abolitionist speech in the years leading up to the Civil War often led to its suppression and the jailing of the speakers. So did speech opposing that war after its commencement. Socialists and anarchists were jailed by the Wilson administration for their speech during World War I. The victims of the House Un-American Activities Committee and the antics of Senator Joseph McCarthy and his colleagues still bear the scars of their mistreatment. More recently, the Obama administration engaged in repeated efforts to punish leakers of information to the press and to limit the ability of journalists to protect their confidential sources. But taken as a whole, the gulf between the legal protections afforded to free expression in the United States and those afforded in Europe remains oceanic.

III

That was not always the case. As late as the 1950s, as Professor Wu has pointed out, "cities or states could ban motion pictures they found distasteful, arrest a man for calling the local sheriff a fascist, and lock up declared members of the Communist Party, all without violating the Constitution." English law on obscenity, as set forth in the 1868 case of *Regina v. Hicklin*, governed in that nation and in the United States well into the twentieth century. Based on its highly repressive test that treated as obscene any work that had a "tendency" to "deprave and corrupt those whose minds are open to such immoral influences," English publishers were jailed for publishing novels of Émile

Zola and works of celebrated authors such as Honoré de Balzac and Gustave Flaubert were banned.

Hicklin was applied in the United States until at least 1933, when the book *Ulysses* was finally admitted into the United States after a memorable district court opinion by Judge James Woolsey followed by an affirmance a year later by the US Court of Appeals for the Second Circuit in an opinion of Judge Augustus Hand that directly criticized English law's "foolish" proscription, a century before, of the works of Lord Byron and Percy Bysshe Shelley. Neither opinion, however, cited the First Amendment, which had not yet been held by the Supreme Court to apply to allegedly obscene works. That did not occur until 1957, when the Supreme Court rejected *Hicklin* as authority on the ground that its test "might well encompass materials legitimately" addressing sexual behavior.

The first and most authoritative rejection in the United States of English law governing expression on First Amendment grounds occurred in 1941, when the Supreme Court all but totally rejected its own ruling thirty-four years earlier in a case involving opinions voiced in newspaper editorials. In 1907, Thomas Patterson was a Denver newspaper publisher who favored municipal-owned and -operated electric power, which could come about only if cities such as Denver were permitted to engage in home rule. Colorado voters voted to amend the state constitution to permit just such home rule. Simultaneously, voters amended the state constitution to provide for additional seats on the state supreme court, with the Colorado governor empowered to appoint them. The lame-duck Republican governor, who had been defeated in his bid for reelection by nine thousand votes, then filled the seats even before they came into existence, and the newly expanded court obligingly held that the governor had, after all, been reelected. That ruling was quickly followed with one holding that the new home rule constitutional amendment was itself unconstitutional. It was, as Wake Forest Law School professor Michael Kent Curtis summarized, "a stolen election in which the state supreme court functioned as an accessory."

In response to the ruling, Patterson published this editorial in his newspaper:

> The people of St. Louis and San Francisco, who have been enjoying the full benefits of just such a system of government as the [home rule] amendment provides, will be astonished to learn that they no longer live in a republic—for the Colorado supreme court holds that such a government is so unrepublican that it cannot be tolerated in Colorado . . . What next? If somebody will let us know what next the utility corporations of Denver and the political machine they control will demand, the question will be answered.

Patterson was held in contempt by the Colorado Supreme Court, the very body he had criticized. From his perspective, as University of Texas Law professor Lucas A. Powe Jr. observed, "no forum could have been worse than the one he got. Whether a Denver jury would have acquitted him may be an open question; that he would have had a chance of acquittal is not."

He fared no better in the US Supreme Court, where Justice Oliver Wendell Holmes wrote the opinion. There, Patterson argued that he was entitled under the First Amendment to publish truthful criticism of the judiciary, just as he could of other government officials. The Court disagreed. According to Justice Holmes, writing for a majority of his colleagues and echoing long-established English law, that missed the point. Truth was irrelevant. What was determinative was that the First Amendment existed primarily to protect against prior restraint of speech, not punishment after it was uttered. "The preliminary freedom," wrote Holmes, "extends as well to the false as to the true; the subsequent punishment may extend as well to the true as to the false."

Holmes addressed the issue of whether judges would or could be unduly influenced by such published advocacy by acknowledging that "judges generally perhaps are less apprehensive that publications impugning their own reasoning or motives will interfere with their administration of the law." Nonetheless, he concluded that "if a court regards, as it may, a publication concerning a matter of law pending before it, as tending toward such an interference, it may punish it" by using its power to hold the speaker or publisher in contempt since "the propriety and necessity of preventing interference with the course of justice by premature statement, argument or intimidation hardly can be denied."

Those views were in all respects consistent with the views expressed by the renowned English scholar William Blackstone in the eighteenth century, with American state cases that echoed Blackstone's views and with two English cases cited by Holmes as if it were self-evident that in this area of law, the law of the mother country guided in that of her doting child as well.

By the time the Court returned to the issue of when speech about pending judicial proceedings could constitutionally lead to a finding of contempt, in *Bridges v. California* in 1941, Holmes was no longer on the Supreme Court. In the intervening years, however, he had starkly changed his views about the First Amendment, writing (mostly in dissent) some of the Supreme Court's most enduring defenses of freedom of speech. But his contempt decision in *Patterson v. Colorado* remained in effect and was applied by the California Supreme Court when a case arose involving an editorial published by the *Los Angeles Times* about a pending application seeking probation by two union members who had been convicted of attacking non-union workers. The three-paragraph editorial was aimed directly at the judge deciding the application.

Two members of Dave Beck's wrecking crew, entertainment committee, goon squad or gorillas, having been convicted in Superior Court of assaulting nonunion truck drivers, have asked for probation. Presumably they will say they are "first offenders," or plead that they were merely indulging a playful exuberance when, with slingshots, they fired steel missiles at men whose only offense was wishing to work for a living without paying tribute to the erstwhile boss of Seattle.

Sluggers for pay, like murderers for profit, are in a slightly different category from ordinary criminals. Men who commit mayhem for wages are not merely violators of the peace and dignity of the State; they are also conspirators against it. The man who burgles because his children are hungry may have some claim on public sympathy. He whose crime is one of impulse may be entitled to lenity. But he who hires out his muscles for the creation of disorder and in aid of a racket is a deliberate foe of organized society and should be penalized accordingly.

It will teach no lesson to other thugs to put these men on good behavior for a limited time. Their "duty" would simply be taken over by others like them. If Beck's thugs, however, are made to realize that they face San Quentin when they are caught, it will tend to make their disreputable occupation unpopular. Judge A. A. Scott will make a serious mistake if he grants probation to Matthew Shannon and Kennan Holmes. This community needs the example of their assignment to the jute mill.

For the California Supreme Court, the issue of whether the newspaper should be held in contempt was not difficult. "Little is said, or can be said," the Court concluded, "in defense of the publication of this editorial." It had gone so far as to name the judge involved; it had explicitly urged him not to grant probation; and the legal issue in the case of whether contempt was a proper remedy had been decided by the Supreme Court in *Patterson*, since what was involved in both cases was a "premature statement, argument, and intimidation" of a judge.

But had Holmes's ruling in *Patterson* sufficiently taken account of the First Amendment? When the US Supreme Court decided the case, it rejected not only *Patterson* but, at least implicitly, its underlying reliance on long-standing English law. Indeed, from a legal perspective, the Court's five-to-four opinion was nothing less than a new declaration of American independence.

Holmes had concluded in *Patterson* that the critical editorial language could "tend to obstruct" and thus interfere with the administration of justice. Justice Hugo Black,
writing for the five-to-four majority of the Court in
Bridges, applied a far more demanding standard, rooted
in another and later formulation by Holmes—the clear
and present danger test. The issue, Black wrote, was nothing less than whether the language posed a "clear and
present danger to the administration of justice." To suppress or punish speech, Black wrote, "the substantive evil
must be extremely serious and the degree of imminence
extremely high."

Holmes had expressed concern in *Patterson* about the
"premature statement" of criticism of the judiciary in the
midst of an ongoing litigation. Black responded that "no
suggestion can be found in the Constitution that the freedom there guaranteed for speech and the press bears an
inverse ratio to the timeliness and importance of the ideas
seeking expression."

Holmes had treated speech critical of judges as potential "intimidation." Black countered by observing that such
a characterization would "impute to judges a lack of firm-
ness, wisdom, or honor."

And, most telling of all, Holmes had relied on well-
established and much-repeated case law that traced its

philosophical roots to English law in effect for hundreds of years. To that, Black responded with a breathtaking conclusion. "No purpose," he wrote, "in ratifying the Bill of Rights was clearer than that of securing for the people of the United States much greater freedom of religion, expression, assembly, and petition than the people of Great Britain had ever enjoyed."

With that audacious, if historically debatable statement, the link between American and English law in the area of freedom of expression was irrevocably broken. Justice Felix Frankfurter, in a passionate dissent in *Bridges* for himself and three other justices, not only denounced what he viewed as Black's simplistic reliance on the First Amendment—"Free speech is not so absolute or irrational a conception as to imply paralysis of the means for effective protection of all the freedoms secured by the Bill of Rights"—but defended English practice through the centuries. "The power exerted by the courts of California," he wrote, "is deeply rooted in the system of administering justice evolved by liberty-loving English-speaking peoples." As for English law itself, Frankfurter emphasized that "since the early eighteenth century, the power to punish for contempt for intrusions into the living process of adjudication has been an unquestioned characteristic of English courts and of the courts of this country."

But for the majority in *Bridges,* and for the Supreme Court in the years that followed, English law was no longer the locale for American judges to visit to receive guidance as to how to apply the First Amendment. America was on its own, and First Amendment law grew ever more expansive and more distinct from that applied abroad.

IV

The chasm between European and American free speech jurisprudence may best be gauged by viewing in some detail the different level of protection each provides in specific areas.

A number of examples have already been described. Another, worthy of more extensive commentary, arises out of the adoption within the European Union of a legally enforceable "right to be forgotten," based upon a 2014 ruling of the European Court of Justice. At the core of the ruling, rooted in an effort to protect personal privacy, is the determination that Google and other search engines must remove links to content initially published in newspapers or elsewhere that reveals information that is now determined to be "inadequate, irrelevant or no longer relevant."

That decision is initially to be made by Google and other search engines with appeals authorized to local data protection authorities if the demanding party is unsatisfied with the decision. Truth is no defense. However accurate the information may have been or remains, it must be removed unless it is determined still to be "relevant." New rules proposed by the European Union to go into effect in 2018 would go further still in empowering subjects of stories or articles to require their deletion. As summarized by the European Commission, the new proposed rules amount to this: "When you no longer want your data to be processed, and provided that there are no legitimate grounds for retaining it, the data will be deleted."

The impact of these provisions has been the subject of ongoing debate. Supporters have sought to minimize their impact on the availability of information. The *Guardian*, for example, has concluded, based on its examination of Google's deletion policy, that more than 95 percent of requests for deletions have come from "everyday members of the public," as opposed to criminals, politicians, and high-profile individuals, and that virtually all deletions have related to "private or personal information." But that begs the question of how those words should be interpreted, since the decision as to what is "personal" or "private" is highly subjective.

Similarly, a *New York Times* article written by Farhad Manjoo, published in 2015, maintained that since the then computed four hundred thousand articles ordered deleted (the number has since risen to more than five hundred thousand) amounted to only a tiny percentage of "the billions of pages online," that it was "difficult to shed many tears" for these articles "that will no longer show up." The author's equanimity, even serenity, about the deletion of so many articles is striking. If Google had been ordered to delete a single previously published review of even an out-of-print book on the ground that the review was no longer "relevant," the outcry from the literary world would have been explosive. It is difficult to accept that such a blasé dismissal of the forced deletion from Google of half a million articles can be justified on arithmetical grounds.

Google itself maintains that having been charged with the unsought responsibility of censoring itself, it considers "the public interest remaining in its search results— for example, if it relates to financial scams, professional malpractice, criminal convictions or your public conduct as a government official." But even such good-faith efforts at enforcing the law and regulations leave the widest range of subjective decisions to be made.

This is particularly well illustrated by reviewing a sample of articles actually deleted from Google. In that respect, the English newspaper the *Telegraph* has performed a significant public service by reviewing which of its own articles have been ordered deleted and by publishing, in September 2015, summaries of one hundred of them. They included articles about the convictions of individuals of crimes, the acquittal of others, various investigations, arrests, and litigations, the conduct of police officers, teachers, and other public employees, and a wide array of conduct deemed to be newsworthy by the newspaper, the publication of which had not been found to violate any English law. Of the hundred deleted articles summarized by the *Telegraph*, I have chosen a sampling of the following twenty-five:

- A story about the jailing of a doctor for six years for attempting to spike his pregnant mistress's drinks with drugs to cause her to miscarry their son. The link concerned was an article detailing an email he sent to a colleague following his arrest.
- An article about a pensioner's body that lay undiscovered in her home in Norwich for up to six months before it was discovered by police. Norfolk coroner

William Armstrong described the case as "deeply disturbing."

- An article about a former porn star and brother of a baroness who was found guilty of two counts of insider trading.
- A story about an army captain who accused her commanding officer of labeling her a "blonde bimbo" and had her claim dismissed by an employment tribunal.
- An article about a Scottish man who was jailed for life for strangling his wife with a tartan tie and hiding her body under their bed for a week.
- A story about a hotel manager who hid £58,000 in stolen cash taken from her employers and recently married couples in bags and boxes under her bed. She was jailed for nine months.
- An article about a pilot who was killed during a fundraising flight for his village church in Dorset during 2009.
- A story about a mother of two who was unanimously found not guilty of seven charges made against her by a sixteen-year-old male pupil, who alleged the pair had a ten-month relationship.
- A story about a "dapper" diamond thief who killed his wife before hanging himself at their home in one of London's most affluent postcodes.
- An article about a company director who killed himself while on Skype with his partner. He was on a business assignment in India when he cut his own throat on camera while talking with his distraught partner in the United Kingdom.

- An article detailing how a Royal Air Force officer
  was accused in a court martial proceeding of sexually
  assaulting a female junior officer after creeping into
  her bedroom following a champagne party. The link
  to a second article following his unanimous acquittal
  a week later has also been removed.
- A 2003 article about people under thirty suffering
  strokes.
- A story about a law student who was convicted of
  killing and burying in concrete his controlling father
  who wanted him to study at the Sorbonne in Paris
  instead of living with his girlfriend in London.
- An article detailing how the Roman Catholic Church
  reached a £15,000 out-of-court settlement with a
  former boy scout who claimed he was abused by a
  friar who was the son of J. R. R. Tolkien, the *Lord
  of the Rings* author.
- An article about a twenty-seven-year-old man who
  was killed in a plane crash in Nepal with six fellow
  British travelers.
- An article about a senior manager at a prominent
  London law firm who wanted to work part-time,
  including half a day a week from home, after having
  a baby and won her claim for unfair dismissal.
- An article about a city trader who confided in his boss
  that he felt suicidal, was told, "Tough luck, dude—pull
  yourself together," and appealed to an employment
  tribunal.
- A story about a detective who sparked an armed siege
  inside a police station after allegedly threatening to
  kill a colleague.

- An article recounting the story of a Kosovo-born Muslim and her fight against deportation from Holland.
- A story about a maid who claimed that she had been beaten and kept as a slave by her employers and who faced prosecution after an employment tribunal ruled that she invented the abuse.
- An article about a leading researcher into heart disease who escaped jail after a court heard that he slapped his fiancée and broke a hotel deputy manager's arm in a drunken rage on the eve of his wedding.
- An article about a director who was jailed for eight years for stealing more than £34 million from a dotcom company.
- A story about a policeman whose assault on a man was filmed by a CCTV camera and who was jailed for twenty-one months.
- A story about a former care assistant in an old people's home who was jailed in 2004 for helping her lover rob elderly women.
- An article about a former world boxing champion who was jailed for two and a half years in 2003 after he was caught with £21,000 worth of cannabis in his car.

All these articles must be assumed to have been accurate or, at the least, nonactionable. Some of them, but by no means all, may seem inconsequential, even unworthy of publication in newspapers that focused less on criminal conduct. And there is no doubt that all of them caused discomfort at some level to those written about or related to those who were. Requests to delete them would not have been made if that were not true.

But taken separately or as a whole, they reflect a bit of the reality of life as depicted in the *Telegraph* through the years in which they were written. As regards most of them, and surely all those involving judicial proceedings, it is less than clear why the articles fall within the rubric of "privacy" at all. Or why they should be viewed as "inadequate, irrelevant or no longer relevant," the EU-imposed test Google is required to apply to delete them.

The crimes described were real; the deaths occurred; the trials transpired. Each article met the journalistic standards applied by the *Telegraph* for what was newsworthy at the time it was published, a standard not properly subject to second-guessing by any government body or edict. Although most of them did not relate to publicly recognized individuals, all related to matters of public interest and often of public concern.

It is not a small thing for a government, let alone a continent-wide governmental entity, to criminalize the dissemination of truthful information on the medium that most people turn to for just such information. But that is now the law in Europe. And it has also been applied to online copies of newspapers that published truthful articles years before. In April 2016, for example, a Belgium superior court ordered a newspaper to delete from a twenty-two-year-old article in its online archives the name of the driver of a car who was in an accident that resulted in two deaths.

The dangers of state-required suppression of truthful information are not limited to Europe. As this book was written, French authorities imposed a fine of $112,000 on Google for failing to remove certain to-be-forgotten materials from its servers in the United States as well. Google will presumably ultimately do what it must to comply with the dictates of the law, but Americans can take both comfort and pride that no American court would or, under the First Amendment, could require it to do so.

V

Another controversial area that deserves separate review relates to how the United States and European nations differ in their treatment of individuals or organizations that wish to participate in political or other public campaigns by spending their money to do so.

In England, an antiabortion organization called the Society for the Protection of the Unborn Child sought to further its cause by distributing one and a half million leaflets contrasting the views of candidates in the 1992 parliamentary election in one district on abortion-related issues. For doing so, the society's executive director, Phyllis Bowman, was charged with the crime of spending more than the statutory limit of £5—$7!—"with a view to promoting or procuring that election of a candidate." She had twice before been convicted of the same crime.

I cannot help but repeat that. It was a crime for an organization with strongly held views about a much-disputed issue of public policy of the greatest moral and political impact to spend a total of more than $7 for the purpose of distributing leaflets supporting or opposing the candidacy of candidates for election to Parliament. And the executive director of the antiabortion organization had twice before been convicted of that crime.

In this case, Bowman was acquitted on a technicality; the summons charging her had not been issued within the statutory limit of one year. Her challenge to the legality of the statute under article 10 of the European Convention on Human Rights, which protects freedom of expression, was nonetheless permitted to continue. According to the European Court of Human Rights, the basis for such a statute was legitimate: it sought to assure equality between candidates, and that interest sufficed to overcome the law's impact on free speech. The minuscule amount she was permitted to spend, however, the Court determined was too small, and the restriction was thus "disproportionate to the aim pursued." Parliament responded by raising the maximum amount that a third party could lawfully expend on an election to £500 pounds (around $700), and that remains the law today. If, within a time period four to six weeks before an election, the society spent more than that amount in preparing and distributing its leaflets, it would have committed a crime.

Such limitations may be imposed throughout Europe not only on spending in elections but on seeking to persuade legislatures to enact (or to determine not to enact) legislation. A ruling of the European Court of Human Rights is illustrative.

Animal Defenders International, a London-based organization that campaigns against various uses of animals in commerce, science, and leisure and that seeks to influence public policy to change legislation that bears on those issues, commenced, in 2005, a campaign called "My Mate's a Primate," which took issue with the keeping and exhibition of primates in television advertising. It sought to broadcast a twenty-second television advertisement expressing its views but was prevented from doing so by a United Kingdom law that flatly prohibited any political advertising.

The claim of the organization that its prepared advertisement should have been aired was dismissed by the English High Court, a ruling that was, in turn, affirmed by the House of Lords, which observed that the ban on such advertising on television had been enacted to assure a "playing field of debate" that would be "so far as practicable level." That objective, Lord Bingham of Cornhill observed in the lead opinion of the House of Lords, was to limit the power of "well-endowed interests which are not political parties ... to use the power of the purse to give enhanced prominence to views which may be true or false, attractive to progressive minds or unattractive, beneficial or injurious." Baroness Hale of Richmond, in her opinion, referred to American practice as the "elephant in the ... room," decrying the enormous amounts spent in American elections and the impact of such advertising on public opinion. "Our democracy," she wrote, "is based upon more than one person one vote. It is based on the view that each person has equal value" and on the accompanying notion that "we want to avoid the grosser distortions which unrestricted access to the broadcast media will bring."

By a nine-to-eight vote, the Grand Chamber of the European Court of Human Rights concluded that there had been no violation of article 10 in the denial of the appeal by the animal rights group. The slim majority afforded considerable deference to the decision of Parliament to adopt the legislation and the absence of any general consensus among European states as to the topic. In good part, it relied on the fact that other media remained open to the animal rights group to present its views. "In particular," the opinion of the court concluded, "it remains open to the applicant ... to participate in radio or television discussion programmes of a political nature (ie. broadcasts other than paid advertisements)." "Importantly," the court observed, "the applicant has full access for its advertisement to non-broadcasting media including the print media, the internet (including social media) as well as to demonstrations, posters and flyers."

A concurring opinion observed, as well, that "there is no dispute that the legislation served [the] legitimate aim ... [of] the protection of the impartiality of public interest broadcasting and the democratic process itself, by ensuring that financially powerful groups were not able directly or indirectly to dictate the political agenda, and thereby making effective the principle of the equality of opportunity."

An American even vaguely aware of First Amendment jurisprudence might think it self-evident that it would be unconstitutional for the government to treat as criminal the conduct of an antiabortion or animal rights group in printing and distributing leaflets setting forth their views about whom to vote for or against or for placing an advertisement on television advocating their cause. But critics of the *Citizens United* case should take care about too quickly endorsing those views. For the same could be said of criminalizing the behavior of a politically engaged group, partially funded by corporate contributions, that sought to place on American television a documentary that was harshly critical of the then leading candidate for the presidential nomination of one of our two major political parties. That, of course, is precisely what was at issue in *Citizens United.*

Citizens United, a case in which I represented Republican Senator Mitch McConnell in the Supreme Court, addressed the question of whether a conservative political group could, without risking criminal penalties, produce and then offer on video-on-demand a documentary described by Justice Kennedy as "in essence . . . a feature-length negative advertisement that urges viewers to vote against Senator [Hillary] Clinton for President." It is one of two Supreme Court rulings, both extremely controversial and both much disapproved of by scholars (as well as, polls indicate, by an overwhelming percentage of the general public), that are facially inconsistent with the European Court rulings summarized above.

One of the determinations in the earlier case, *Buckley v. Valeo,* would plainly have protected Bowman as she distributed her leaflets. In *Buckley,* decided in 1976, the Court concluded that "a restriction on the amount of money a person or group can spend on political communication during a campaign necessarily reduces the quantity of expression by restricting the number of issues discussed, the depth of their exploration, and the size of the audience reached." It responded to the claim that too much money in politics led to too much "bad" or negative speech in elections by concluding that "the First Amendment denies government the power to determine that spending to promote one's political views is wasteful, excessive, or unwise. In the free society ordained by our Constitution, it is not the government, but the people—individually, as citizens and candidates, and collectively, as associations and political committees—who must retain control over the quantity and range of debate on public issues in a political campaign." And in *Buckley*, the Court concluded, in much-quoted words, as follows: "The concept that government may restrict the speech of some elements of our society in order to enhance the relative voice of others is wholly foreign to the First Amendment, which was designed 'to secure "the widest possible dissemination of information from diverse and antagonistic sources,"' and '"to assure unfettered exchange of ideas for the bringing about of political and social changes desired by the people."'"

Buckley thus held that just as individuals could speak as

often as they were able to in person or in writing in support of candidates for public office, they could spend whatever amounts they chose to purchase the advertisements that contained that speech. And *Citizens United*, in turn, held that corporations could do the same.

Should the fact that what was involved in these cases was money lead to a different result? "Of course," UCLA Law professor Eugene Volokh has observed, "money isn't speech. But so what? The question is not whether money is speech, but whether the First Amendment *protects our right to speak using your money.*" "After all," Volokh said, "money isn't lawyering, but the Sixth Amendment secures criminal defendants' right to hire a lawyer. Money isn't contraception or abortions, but people have a right to buy condoms or pay doctors to perform abortions. Money isn't education, but people have a right to send their children to private schools. Money isn't speech, but people have a right to spend money to publish *The New York Times*. Money isn't religion (at least not for most of us), but people have a right to donate money to their church."

The first law to bar corporations and unions from using their funds to make independent expenditures designed to affect federal elections was the Taft-Hartley Act, adopted in 1947. Contributions by corporations to candidates had been barred since 1907, but not until the adoption of Taft-Hartley were independent expenditures—that is, money spent supporting a candidate in a manner unco-ordinated with him or her—deemed criminal. From its adoption, the constitutionality of the statute was viewed as dubious. President Harry S. Truman vetoed the bill on the ground that it was a "dangerous intrusion on free speech."

The constitutionality of the new provisions was quickly questioned by the Supreme Court in *United States v. CIO*, in which the Court concluded that unless read extremely narrowly, "the gravest doubt would arise in our minds as to [the statute's] constitutionality." In that case and in the Court's later ruling in *United States v. Auto Workers*, the more liberal members of the Court concluded that the statute was facially inconsistent with the First Amend-ment. In the former case, Justices Wiley Rutledge, Hugo Black, William O. Douglas, and Frank Murphy, probably the four most liberal jurists ever to sit on the Supreme Court at the same time, concluded that whatever "undue influence" was obtained by making large expenditures was outweighed by "the loss for democratic processes result-ing from the restrictions upon free and full public discus-sion." In the *Auto Workers* case, a dissenting opinion by Justice Douglas (joined by Chief Justice Earl Warren and

Justice Black) even more clearly presaged the later ruling of Justice Kennedy in *Citizens United*, concluding:

> Some may think that one group or another should not express its views in an election because it is too powerful, because it advocates unpopular ideas, or because it had a record of lawless action. But these are not justifications for withholding First Amendment rights from any group—labor or corporate. . . . First Amendment rights are part of the heritage of all persons and groups in this country. They are not to be dispensed or withheld merely because we or the Congress thinks the person or group is worthy or unworthy.

Justice Kennedy's analysis in *Citizens United* was rooted in two well-established legal propositions. The first, that political speech—not to say political speech about whom to vote for or against—is at the core of the First Amendment, is hardly novel. First Amendment theorists have occasionally debated how far beyond political speech the amendment's protection should be understood to go, but there has never been doubt that generally, as Justice Kennedy put it, "political speech must prevail against laws that would suppress it by design or inadvertence." Nor has it been disputed that, as Justice Kennedy stated, the First Amendment "'has its fullest and most urgent application' to speech uttered during a campaign for political office."

The second critical prong of Justice Kennedy's opinion addressed the issue of whether the fact that Citizens United was a corporation could deprive it of the right to endorse candidates by making independent expenditures that individuals had long since been held to have. In holding that the corporate status of an entity could not negate this right, Justice Kennedy cited twenty-five cases of the Court in which corporations had received full First Amendment protection. Many of them involved powerful newspapers owned by large corporations; others involved non-press entities such as a bank, a real estate company, and a public utility company. Justice Stevens's dissenting opinion (but not most of the published criticism of the *Citizens United* ruling) took no issue with this historical record, acknowledging that "we have long since held that corporations are covered by the First Amendment."

The inherent First Amendment dangers of any statute barring close-to-election speech advocating the election or defeat of candidates for office were starkly illustrated during questioning by the Justices of counsel for the United States. While the statutes at issue in *Citizens United* only applied to speech that was on television, cable, and satellite, the logic of the government's position appeared to lead inexorably to the proposition that books funded by corporations or unions and published close to elections could as well constitutionally be banned if Congress determined that their impact was too great. Deputy Solicitor General Malcolm Stewart, arguing for the government in March 2009, did his best to avoid that issue but finally—and honorably—gave up the ghost:

> JUSTICE KENNEDY: Just to make it clear, it's the government's position that under the statute, if this [K]indle device where you can read a book which is campaign advocacy, within the 60–30 day period, if it comes from a satellite, it's under—it can be prohibited under the Constitution and perhaps under this statute?
>
> MR. STEWART: It—it can't be prohibited, but a corporation could be barred from using its general treasury funds to publish the book and could be required to use—to raise funds to publish the book using its PAC.

And then this:

> CHIEF JUSTICE ROBERTS: Take my hypothetical. [A book] doesn't say at the outset. It funds—here is—whatever it is, this is a discussion of the American political system, and at the end it says vote for X.
>
> MR. STEWART: Yes, our position would be that the corporation could be required to use PAC funds rather than general treasury funds.
>
> CHIEF JUSTICE ROBERTS: And if they didn't, you could ban it?
>
> MR. STEWART: If they didn't, we could prohibit the

publication of the book using the corporate treasury funds.

At the reargument six months later, then-Solicitor General (now Supreme Court Justice) Elena Kagan was well prepared to deal with the uproar that followed Stewart's response. She did so by seeking to draw a different line, arguing that while one section of the statute at issue, which also limited corporate and union expenditures, could cover "full-length books," there would be a "quite good as-applied challenge" were it used in that manner. Here was her best shot in response to a question she surely anticipated more than any other: Could books be banned under the government's theory or not?

GENERAL KAGAN: [W]e took what the Court—what the Court's—the Court's own reaction to some of those other hypotheticals [about books] very seriously. We went back, we considered the matter carefully, and the government's view is that although 441b [of a related law] does cover full-length books, that there would be [a] quite good as-applied challenge to any attempt to apply 441b in that context.

And I should say that the FEC has never applied 441b in that context. So for 60 years a book has never been at issue.

JUSTICE SCALIA: What happened to the overbreadth doctrine? I mean, I thought our doctrine in the [First]

Amendment is if you write it too broadly, we are not going to pare it back to the point where it's constitutional. If it's overbroad, it's invalid. What has happened to that[?]

GENERAL KAGAN: I don't think that it would be substantially overbroad, Justice Scalia, if I tell you that the FEC has never applied this statute to a book. To say that it doesn't apply to books is to take off, you know, essentially nothing.

CHIEF JUSTICE ROBERTS: But we don't put our—we don't put our First Amendment rights in the hands of FEC bureaucrats; and if you say that you are not going to apply it to a book, what about a pamphlet?

GENERAL KAGAN: I think a—a pamphlet would be different. A pamphlet is a pretty classic electioneering, so there is no attempt to say that 441b only applies to video and not to print.

Both lawyers for the United States did precisely what the best Supreme Court advocates attempt to do when confronted with questions that expose the weakest link in their argument—try to provide some comfort to the Court that the likelihood of any potentially harmful societal impact of their position actually occurring was minimal. Both were, at the same time, candid with the Court, Stewart conceding that the government's position on the constitutionality of the statute could (at least in theory) justify a ban on books as well and Kagan acknowledging that the text of one relevant section of law already covered books. But their answers—Stewart seeking to provide constitutional justification for the banning of books, Kagan attempting the same with respect to pamphlets—are hopeless. No relevant constitutional distinction can be drawn between books and pamphlets, and no distinction in this area between both books and pamphlets and broadcast and cable makes any sense at all.

One might have thought that the press, dependent as it is on expansive First Amendment protection, would support such a First Amendment protective ruling with respect to speech about elections. The press had celebrated one case, *Mills v. Alabama,* decided in 1966, in which the Supreme Court unanimously held unconstitutional a state statute that, in the name of electoral purity and simple fairness, had applied to the press a law that barred on election day only, "any electioneering . . . in support of or in opposition to any proposition" being voted on by the public. In that case, the Court had concluded that no statute could limit, even for a day, what the press printed about an election, however unfair its coverage or how great the impact of its publication. "There is," the Court said, "practically universal agreement that a major purpose of [the First] Amendment was to protect the free discussion of government affairs . . . of candidates . . . and all . . . matters relating to political processes." That being so, no limitations on expression, such as Alabama had imposed, could survive First Amendment scrutiny.

In another press-freedom case, *Miami Herald Publishing Co. v. Tornillo,* decided in 1974, the Court, again unanimously, determined that a Florida law that required newspapers that had criticized political candidates to provide equal space for responses was facially inconsistent with the First Amendment. Government coercion of this sort, the Court held, "brings about a confrontation with the express provisions of the First Amendment" since legislative restrictions on advocacy for or against political candidates are at odds with the guarantees of the First Amendment.

Both of these rulings raised similar issues to those raised by critics of the Roberts Court's campaign finance rulings. In both, critics of press power and behavior relied on what they urged were democratic principles to overcome the ability of the press to determine for itself what to print and what not.

Why, the proponents of the Alabama legislation asked, at a time when most people received their news from a single newspaper in a community in which there was no other, was it not fairer and more likely to lead to more thoughtful decisions by voters to bar, on election day only, advocacy as to how to vote? Why, in fact, was it not more democratic to do so rather than running the risk that the newspaper would have too great an impact on the election by offering, on election day, "last minute political charges without opportunity to answer"?

And why, the proponents in Florida of its right to reply statute asked, was it not fairer and more democratic to permit someone accused by a newspaper of some sort of misconduct to reply to the charges? Why was the Florida Supreme Court wrong in concluding that since the statute was "designed to add to the flow of information and ideas" and simply required "in the interest of full and fair discussion, additional information," it was consistent with the First Amendment?

In both cases, the Court rejected out-of-hand the argument that freedom of expression could be limited in the name of democracy. In both, it seemed so obvious to the Court—both rulings were unanimous—that either legislatively limiting what the press could say or requiring it to say things it chose not to was so inherently *undemocratic* that doing so could not possibly be deemed consistent with the First Amendment. Yet if full and free discussions of all matters relating to elections could not be limited even for a brief time by legislation purportedly adopted to assure fairness in elections (as *Mills* concluded) and the expression of *more* views about whom to vote for could not be legislatively required (as in *Tornillo*), it is difficult to conclude that the government may limit the amount of speech deemed lawful by limiting the amount of money that may be spent to pay for the dissemination of that speech. It is thus hardly surprising that both the *Mills* and *Tornillo* cases were cited and relied on by the Supreme Court in *Buckley*.

But leading press entities continue to decry the rulings in *Buckley* and *Citizens United*, even as their own freedom to speak about candidates and elections as they choose and to spend however much they choose (or are able) to spend in that regard is unlimited.

A telling example surfaced after Supreme Court Justice Samuel Alito spoke at a Federalist Society event in 2012 and pointed out that in cases involving the press, the Supreme Court had long since established that media corporations possessed sweeping First Amendment rights. "The question," he said, "is whether speech that goes to the very heart of government should be limited to certain preferred corporations: namely, media corporations." The very idea, he urged, "that the First Amendment protects only certain privileged voices should be disturbing to anybody who believes in free speech."

The response of the *New York Times* was one of consternation. The press was protected, it argued in an edito-

rial, not because it operated in corporate form but because of its function, "the vital role that the press plays in
American democracy." Quoting from Justice Stevens's
dissent in *Citizens United*, the *Times* urged that when the
Bill of Rights was drafted, "it was the free speech of individual Americans that they had in mind," not that of corporations. According to the *Times*, the *Citizens United* majority had "never explained why any corporation that does
not have a press function warrants the same free speech
rights as a person."

Two responses may be offered to the *Times*'s myopic
position. The first is that Justice Alito had not urged that
the press received First Amendment protection *because* it
utilized the corporate form. What the justice had argued
was that the fact that the *Times* and other journalistic entities were owned by corporations was *irrelevant* to their
receiving full First Amendment protection, precisely what
the Supreme Court concluded in *Citizens United*.

The second is that the *Times*'s editorial fully, if inadver-
tently, vindicated Justice Alito's submission that it viewed
itself as "preferred" in that it could exist in corporate form
and receive full First Amendment protection while nonmedia corporations could not. So if the *Times* had its way,
the plethora of noncommercial entities that are organized as corporations but do not have a "press function"—

universities, museums, theaters, bookstores, and not-for-profit entities such as the American Civil Liberties Union and the National Rifle Association that take positions on public issues—would no longer have First Amendment protection.

As for nonmedia corporations, if the *Times*'s position were correct, as Brooklyn Law School professor Joel Gora has observed, its corporate owners could "endorse a presidential candidate on page twenty-six" while "the corporate owners of General Motors" could be held criminally liable for publishing an ad with the identical message on page twenty-five. Or for publishing a message that disagreed with that of the *Times*.

Similarly, the *Times* could publish an editorial denouncing a corporation for the vilest sort of misconduct imperiling the safety of its employees, but if the corporation responded by publishing its version of an op-ed piece responding to the charges, the corporation would receive no First Amendment protection at all. That was precisely the issue raised in the *Nike v. Kasky* case commenced in California against Nike. The company had been accused, in press releases, newspaper editorials, and the like, of having subjected its workers abroad to brutal working conditions. Nike denied the charges and responded in a variety of ways, including issuing press releases, publishing a pamphlet defending its conduct, and writing a letter to the editor of the *Times*. The company was sued in California state court for that speech under a state consumer protection statute that barred false advertising and the like. The legal issue was straightforward: How much First Amendment protection, if any, did the First Amendment afford Nike? The California Supreme Court concluded that the protection was significantly limited, just as a commercial advertisement by Nike would have been. The US Supreme Court declined to decide the issue because the case had not been finally determined by the California courts.

But the *New York Times*, in a friend-of-the-court brief it filed with the Supreme Court together with other newspapers and media entities in 2002, had no difficulty in concluding that Nike, a nonmedia corporation, was entitled to sweeping First Amendment protection for its speech. In unambiguous language, the *Times*'s brief told the Court that "businesses and their representatives have just as much a right to speak out on any public issue as do interest groups and politicians, whose motivations for speaking are often just as selfish and whose reputations for unadorned veracity are often just as suspect." And that "because issues concerning companies' 'business operations' are increasingly fundamental to the world's social and political landscape, the withdrawal of corporate voices on these issues from the media would deprive the public of vital information." Nothing has changed in the intervening years to make those statements any less compelling.

The treatment of purely commercial speech raises a related issue. Historically, purely commercial speech has received lesser First Amendment protection than speech related to public issues. That remains a much-disputed area of law. What has never been disputed, though, is that such limitations as have been placed on false or misleading commercial speech have not been adopted because of the corporate status of the speaker but because of the topic of the speech. Individuals are limited in their commercial speech (and protected under the First Amendment when they engage in such speech) to the same degree as are corporations. There is no reason, as the *Times* and the press generally previously understood, why that should not continue to be the case with respect to the commentary of all on matters of public interest.

Money does matter enormously, of course, but not in the way and certainly not to the extent that some in the press have claimed. When the *Citizens United* ruling was issued, the *Times* foresaw that its effect would be to "thrust politics back to the robber-baron era of the 19th century" by allowing "corporations to use their vast treasuries to overwhelm elections"; the *Washington Post* warned that "corporate money, never lacking in the American political process, may now overwhelm . . . the contributions of individuals"; and the *San Francisco Chronicle* declared that "voters should prepare for the worst: cash-drenched elections presided over by free-spending corporations." Every one of these predictions has turned out to be inaccurate.

As of February 9, 2016, the *Times* itself reported that fifty-seven contributions to super PACs in excess of a million dollars had been made. Of them only five were from corporations, ranging from the $10 million donation from C. V. Starr and Company, a company run by Maurice Greenberg, the former CEO of AIG, to $1.3 million by American Pacific International Capital, a diversified holding company whose board of directors included one of Jeb Bush's younger brothers. The other three corporate contributors included one privately held holding company ($2.8 million), one horse stable ($2.5 million), and one private investment firm ($2.3 million). Additionally, thirty donations of an even $1 million had been made. Of those, only three were corporations. In all, then, of the eighty-seven million-dollar or million-dollar-plus contributors to super PACs, only eight were from corporations, none of them of enormous size.

There remains the issue of secrecy, of "dark money" from contributors, including corporations, not disclosed to the public. How, as David Ignatius put it in an otherwise subtle and thoughtful article in the *Washington Post* in 2016, could the Supreme Court in *Citizens United* have produced an opinion that reflected an "unfortunate refusal to limit secret money"? The Court did just the opposite, ruling by an eight-to-one vote that the disclosure requirements of the campaign finance law at issue in the case were constitutional. Its opinion could hardly have been clearer, stating that "the First Amendment protects political speech; and disclosure permits citizens and shareholders to react to the speech of corporate entities in a proper way . . . [by] enabl[ing] the electorate to make informed decisions and give proper weight to different speakers and messages."

Nor was it the *Citizens United* ruling or the Supreme Court that has permitted the nondisclosure of the identity of any contributors or the amount of their expenditures or contributions. It has been the Internal Revenue Service and a complicit Congress, which, in contradiction to the language of one section of federal law (Section 501 (c)(4)) has permitted a significant amount of electoral expenditures to be made by tax-exempt "social welfare" organizations. Moreover, as summarized by the Center for Competitive Politics in 2015, under Federal Communications Commission regulations, all broadcast and cable political advertisements must contain the name of the entity paying for the ad; all print political ads must contain the name of the payer; and "candidates, political parties, PACs, and Super PACs at the federal level and in 49 states must disclose their expenditures, income, and donors." Of the over $7 billion spent on federal races in 2012, less than $311 million was "dark money," about 4.4 percent of total spending, and most of that came from organizations such as the US Chamber of Commerce, the League of Conservation Voters, the National Rifle Association, Planned Parenthood, and the like. It may well be true, as noted earlier, that the IRS has erred in allowing the sources of donations to those organizations to remain undisclosed. But that failure can hardly be laid at the doors of the Supreme Court or its *Citizens United* ruling.

Journalistic predictions about the impact of money on the 2016 campaign have been similarly flawed. A typical prediction was that of the *Times* on July 31, 2015, before the first scheduled Republican debate that year, that the debate might provide "entertainment and conflict" but that the "circus will probably have little effect on the race" as compared to the appearances of some of the candidates before the Koch brothers and their colleagues seeking their financial support. In every respect, that prediction proved to be inaccurate. Wisconsin governor Scott Walker, extremely well funded from the start, quickly fell so far behind others that he was obliged to abandon the race before a single primary had occurred. The same was true of former Texas governor Rick Perry. Florida's Jeb Bush and New Jersey's Chris Christie spent more money in New Hampshire than any other candidates but did so poorly that they had to withdraw from the race. Others who began with still more limited funding—Senator Bernie Sanders of Vermont for one—played major roles in the campaign.

It is not as if nothing has happened as a result of the *Buckley* and *Citizens United* rulings. Although the degree of augmented corporate involvement in elections has been vastly overstated, very wealthy individuals and families have spent far more than was ever previously the case in support of candidates they favored, money that *Buckley* permitted them to spend but that it was unclear, until post–*Citizens United* rulings, if they could do so together with others. There is no doubt that by doing so, those people assured themselves of greater access to the political candidates they supported than is available to others. That is one of the main objections to *Citizens United* that critics of it have repeatedly voiced and it is accurate.

But the notion that such access amounts to some sort of corruption is less than clear. As Justice Kennedy had observed in an earlier case and repeated in *Citizens United*,

"It is in the nature of an elected representative to favor certain policies, and, by necessary corollary, to favor the voters and contributors who support those policies. It is well understood that a substantial and legitimate reason, if not the only reason, to cast a vote for, or to make a contribution to, one candidate over another is that the candidate will respond by producing those political outcomes the supporter favors." The Supreme Court went even further in its 2016 ruling, reversing the corruption conviction of former Virginia governor Robert McDonnell, unanimously concluding that "significant constitutional concerns" would be raised if a public official could be at risk of a criminal indictment if a union had contributed to his or her campaign and after the election the official arranged meetings for it and contacted other officials on its behalf. "The basic compact," the Court declared, "underlying representative government *assumes* that public officials will hear from their constituents and act appropriately on their concerns."

In fact, expenditures by supporters of one candidate or the other in the 2016 Republican primary campaign for the presidency had at least one strikingly beneficial, and profoundly prodemocratic, result. More candidates sought the Republican nomination for president in 2016 than in living memory. There were more candidates for the public to choose from and more public engagement and involvement in the race than had been the case for decades. That Donald J. Trump, the victor, spent considerably less than many of his competitors proves little in light of the staggering amount of free television and cable coverage of his campaign. But whatever else may be said about that campaign, his sixteen opponents had their chance to prevail, the money that was expended on their campaigns gave them the wherewithal to do so, and they failed to do so.

Even to cite such sums, however, identifies a broader issue. Only the most minuscule percentage of the public have the sort of money that can actually influence political campaigns. While the 2.5 million contributors to the 2016 campaign of Senator Sanders who contributed, according to the senator, an average of $27 each to his campaign, raised extraordinary sums for his campaign, that outpouring of funds was so exceptional in nature that it can hardly be the basis for the formulation of public policy. Money, as Senator Sanders has emphasized, matters enormously in political campaigns, and the vast income disparity in the nation thus inevitably favors the wealthy.

What need *not* follow from that conclusion, though, is that a proper response is to limit the amount of speech in political campaigns. Economic issues require economic responses, not speech-limiting ones. Without limiting First Amendment rights, Congress and state legislatures may adopt the widest range of legislation to deal with income inequality ranging from higher taxes on the wealthy to higher minimum wages for the least prosperous. Problems of low voter turnout might be dealt with by legislative measures aimed at making it easier to vote and not more difficult or even, as some scholars have urged, compulsory voting. More disclosure about the amount of contributions and the identity of contributors can be required, consistent with the Supreme Court's conclusions in *Citizens United*. More public funding of elections, without limiting private involvement, could assure that more candidates run for office and have a credible chance of success.

Many of these proposals are controversial. Some, however worthy, may simply be impossible at this time given the current state of American politics. Congress and many states may well continue to resist any efforts to expand the electorate, to make it easier for citizens to vote, and to make voting more meaningful. Public support for any such policy changes may now be lacking. But these multifaceted problems should and can be addressed by considering these and other ways of assuring greater public participation in the electoral process rather than by limiting speech itself.

From the date of its release, *Citizens United* has been denounced repeatedly and is surely one of the most unpopular cases with the public ever decided by the Supreme Court. One poll indicates that 80 percent of the public disagrees with the ruling, on an across-the-board bipartisan basis. In part, this may be because of the apocalyptic and never retracted false predictions from many in the press about its likely impact. Was the *New York Times* correct in its editorial declaration that the ruling would return the nation to robber-baron times of the past? Was the *Washington Post's* prediction correct that corporate expenditures would overwhelm those of individuals? Have we really reached a state, as predicted by the *San Francisco Chronicle*, of "cash-drenched elections presided over by free-spending corporations"? *Citizens United* remains a fit topic for debate, but as noted earlier, predictions such as these have been so wide of the mark that they should at least lead readers to approach the topic with a healthy dose of skepticism about those publications' currently expressed views on the subject.

And those of others as well. That the assault on the ruling was so intemperate and came from so many sources added to the sense that the ruling was not only wrongheaded but a juridical disgrace. What else could one conclude when scholars such as Richard L. Hasen, perhaps the nation's leading expert on election law, dismissed views expressed in the ruling as reading "more like the rantings of a right-wing talk show host than the rational view of a justice with a sense of political realism." Or in light of the overheated reaction of the distinguished scholar and philosopher Ronald Dworkin, who would not even accept that the opinion was written in good faith but stemmed from the Court's "instinctive favoritism of corporate interests" or a simple desire to help the Republican Party?

And what else could one make of the opinion based on the comments of journalists such as Howard Fineman, speaking on MSNBC, who characterized the ruling as "one of the most amazing pieces of alleged jurisprudence that I've read." Or, I suppose I must report, of then-MSNBC commentator Keith Olbermann, who weighed in with a bit of personal criticism of me, saying that I would "go down in the history books as the Quisling of freedom of speech in this country" for having represented Senator Mitch McConnell in the case.

Public debate about the case has also been skewed for political reasons. President Obama, a former professor of constitutional law, criticized the legitimacy of the ruling in his 2011 State of the Union address, omitting any reference to its First Amendment roots and inaccurately stating that it would permit money from foreign sources to determine the results of American elections. Democrats have trumpeted what they believe are the failings of the ruling and raised significant sums of money in doing so. Republicans have rarely defended the decision publicly, believing that it favored them and seeing no benefit to them in debating it.

Citizens United speaks for itself. The majority opinion of Justice Kennedy sets forth in detail its underlying basis, one attacked at length in Justice Stevens's lengthy dissenting opinion. What may well be the strongest defense of the ruling, however, was written twenty years before in a dissenting opinion of Justice Scalia. In 1990, the Supreme Court affirmed the constitutionality of a Michigan law that barred corporations from spending their treasury funds to support or oppose candidates running for election in the state. By a six-to-three vote, in *Austin v. Michigan Chamber of Commerce*, the Supreme Court held the statute to be constitutional on the ground that it properly sought to avoid "the corrosive and distorting effects of immense aggregations of wealth that are accumulated with the help of the corporate form and that have little or no correlation to the public's support for the corporation's political ideas."

That ruling (and that basis for it) was rejected by the Court in *Citizens United*. In doing so, Justice Kennedy's opinion relied on a number of rulings of the Court affording broad First Amendment rights for corporations. Most of all, though, the ruling relied upon the language and theme of *Buckley* that had rejected the notion that "the Government has an interest in 'equalizing the relative ability of individuals and groups to influence the outcome of elections.'" "If the First Amendment has any force," Justice Kennedy wrote, "it prohibits Congress from fining or jailing citizens, or associations of citizens, for simply engaging in political speech."

Justice Scalia's dissenting opinion in *Austin* is especially worth recalling. It is that opinion which led me to change my mind about the constitutionality of government-imposed limitations on political expenditures and ultimately to represent Senator Mitch McConnell in *Citizens United* itself. "The Court," Scalia wrote, "today endorses the principle that too much speech is an evil that the democratic majority can proscribe." That principle, he wrote, was "incompatible with the absolutely central truth of the First Amendment: that government cannot be trusted to assure, through censorship, the 'fairness' of political debate."

The Scalia dissent concluded with this peroration:

> The premise of our system is that there is no such thing as too much speech—that the people are not foolish but intelligent, and will separate the wheat from the chaff. As conceded in Lincoln's aphorism about fooling "all of the people some of the time," that premise will not invariably accord with reality; but it will assuredly do so much more frequently than the premise the Court today embraces: that a healthy democratic system can survive the legislative power to prescribe how much political speech is too much, who may speak, and who may not.
>
> Because today's decision is inconsistent with unrepudiated legal judgments of our Court, but even more because it is incompatible with the unrepealable political wisdom of our First Amendment, I dissent.

Readers may not be persuaded, as I was, by the dissenters in *Austin*. Or, as I am, by the majority opinion in *Citizens United*. But they should at least be prepared to acknowledge that on this issue, while many deeply believe that too much money spent on elections by too few people or entities is an assault on democracy itself, others believe, with at least the same good faith, that government should not and may not seek to limit the amount of electoral speech that may be permitted and that the First Amendment precludes it from doing so.

VI

Having sweeping First Amendment rights does not begin
to answer the question of how to use them. The question
of when and what to publish and at what potential social
cost is not always an obvious one.

The decision of the *New York Times* in 1971 to publish
portions of what became known as the Pentagon Papers
did not come easily. Prepared during the war in Vietnam
at the request of Secretary of Defense Robert McNamara
to assess how the United States had become involved in
the war, every one of the three thousand pages of text and
four thousand pages of documents responding to that
query was duly labeled TOP SECRET. In an article I wrote

for the *New York Times Magazine* ten years after the case was decided, I described the decision to publish portions of the study—the *Times* determined not to publish portions of it after consultation with former Defense and State Department officials—as "wrenching." On the one hand, I wrote, the study showed "an extraordinary level of government duplicity" about how and why the nation had become involved in the war; on the other, publishing such documents during the war itself necessarily raised difficult issues as to the national security implications of doing so, as well as significant legal risk for the newspaper itself. "The debate within the paper," I wrote, "was long, exhaustive and sometimes acrimonious" as "executives, editors, reporters and attorneys argued over the meaning of patriotism and journalistic ethics and over the risks of that publication."

The world has changed considerably since those days of journalistic introspection. The seven-thousand-page leak of the Pentagon Papers was shocking for its time, the largest one in American history. Now the leaks of computerized documents relate to millions of pages, as was the situation with Edward Snowden. And the decisions about what to publish relate to far more sensitive revelations. Consider the Snowden documents. I have no doubt that, if someone with his high security clearance had offered to the press in 1971, when the Pentagon Papers were published, documents showing that the US government had engaged in pervasive public deception about how the nation had come to be involved in the Vietnamese war, the *New York Times* and the *Washington Post* would have published that story. In fact, that is just what they did. But I have considerable doubt that either newspaper would have published such revelations as those in the Snowden-provided documents: that the United States routinely listened to the private telephonic communications of the then equivalents of Chancellor Angela Merkel of Germany or President Dilma Rousseff of Brazil. Even less likely would have been the publication by leading American newspapers of Snowden-released documents demonstrating that the United States had intercepted Russian president Dmitry Medvedev's satellite phone or had cooperated with Swedish and Norwegian intelligence services that were engaged in surveillance of Russia. Indeed, if, in 1971, a government official or outside contractor (there was no such thing then) with the equivalent of Snowden's level of security clearance had offered to virtually any American newspaper access to vast amounts of documents classified at or over top-secret level relating to American surveillance or spying abroad, I think it likely the offer would have been declined.

If I am right about this, the change in attitude it reflects may stem from a number of overlapping new realities. American journalists today are no less devoted to their country than those a generation ago. But they are increasingly mistrustful of its government, even when the government claims that publication will do considerable harm. This is the result not only of a generation of government officials crying wolf about the publication of materials that, in retrospect, appeared to have led to no harm at all but of a change in attitude about the role of American journalists in reporting about their country.

Consider the coverage of the *New York Times* when, on June 11, 1940, it reported on Italy's attack on France, an event that President Roosevelt characterized as a "stab in the back." On page 1, a headline of the *Times* read "OUR HELP PLEDGED." Or of the *Times*'s coverage on December 8, 1941, of the Japanese attack on Pearl Harbor, the headline of which read "Tokyo Bombers Strike Hard at Our Main Bases on Oahu." Or the headline on April 13, 1945, which read "Our Okinawa Guns Down 118 Planes." Or the headline, five years later, on June 28, 1950, after the Korean conflict began, that read "OUR FLIERS IN ACTION."

Not long afterward, according to the recollections of longtime *New York Times* editors, the all but familial use in the paper of first-person plural references to the United States or its armed forces—the words "we" and "our," in particular—had ended. A determination had been made that such language constituted what one senior editor referred to as "an unwelcome departure from journalistic detachment."

There is an additional factor. The very existence of the Internet assures that if one newspaper or website declines to publish something, it will nonetheless inevitably appear elsewhere. A decision to publish sensitive materials may thus be defended, correctly or not, as not itself imperiling anything since it is all but certain that the material will, in any event, be made public.

Decisions about what to publish and, more difficult still, what not to publish, have long resulted in internal conflict within American publications. As they should. Decisions about how to reconcile the role of a reporter as a dispassionate observer with his or her relationship with and even loyalty to their country—the very issues that divided so many *New York Times* journalists and executives as they decided whether to publish the Pentagon Papers and, if so, which revelations in them—are similarly inevitable. And they are similarly difficult.

Consider, by way of example, a hypothetical scenario offered on television in 1987, about a decade after the end of the war in Vietnam. It was one of those superb exchanges in the Fred Friendly series called "Ethics in America." With the Vietnam War still fresh in the minds of all participants, the program addressed a number of issues, including the views of the press about its own role in covering a war in which the United States was a participant.

The panel was filled with luminaries. General William Westmoreland, the former commander of American forces in Vietnam, participated actively. So did three more of the best-known individuals in the nation—General Brent Scowcroft, the former national security adviser to Presidents Gerald Ford and George H. W. Bush, and journalists Mike Wallace of *60 Minutes* and Peter Jennings, then the anchor of *World News Tonight* on ABC. The moderator— interrogator—was Charles Ogletree, professor at Harvard Law School. The hypothetical involved a war in a country called Kosan, in which the United States sided with the South Kosanese against the North Kosanese. After raising a number of questions about torture during the Vietnamese conflict, Ogletree turned to the two journalists.

The American media, in the hypothetical, had been asking for some time for access to North Kosan. And the response to Peter Jennings, after long delays, was finally that they could go. He could bring his film crew and they would show him, they said, areas where American and South Kosanese troops had engaged in war crimes. Ogletree asked him, "Would you go?" "Sure," Jennings replied, "absolutely." When he arrived there, the North Kosanese changed the focus of what they were offering. They said, "You know what, we're going to do an ambush tonight of South Kosanese troops. Would you like to accompany us? Bring your cameras, show your public what's going on here." Ogletree asked Jennings, "Would you go?" "Sure." The ambush was set, the North Kosanese troops awaited the arrival of the soldiers they would ambush, and as the other troops got closer and closer, Jennings could make out that it was not just South Kosanese but South Kosanese and American troops on a joint mission together.

Ogletree asked him, "What would you do? Would the filming proceed as you planned?" Jennings sat silently for fifteen seconds, a television eternity. He finally said, "I guess I wouldn't. I am going to tell you now what I am feeling, rather than the hypothesis I drew for myself. If I were with a North Kosanese unit that came upon Americans, I think I personally would do what I could to warn the Americans." "Even if you lost the story?" Ogletree asked. "Even though it would almost certainly mean losing my life," Jennings answered. "But I do not think that I could bring myself to participate in that act. That's purely personal, and other reporters might have a different reaction."

Mike Wallace did. He said, "I think some other reporters *would* have a different reaction." They would, he said, view it as a story they were there to cover. Wallace turned to Jennings and admonished him. "I'm astonished," he said. "Peter, I am astonished. You are a reporter. Granted, you're an American, but I'm at a little bit of a loss to understand why, because you're an American [Jennings happened to be Canadian], you would not have covered that story."

Ogletree then asked Wallace, "Don't you think you have some sort of higher duty in a situation in which American troops are involved to warn them?" "No," Wallace said, "you don't have a higher duty."

Jennings retreated. "I chickened out," he said. "I wish I had made another decision. I would like to have made his decision"—referring to Wallace's statement that he would have kept on filming.

One of the panelists was a marine colonel who had served in Vietnam. Glaring at the journalists, his voice filled with scorn, he expanded the hypothetical. He said the following: "A few days after the ambush you guys are going to be back on our side. And one of you may get wounded walking around there and I'm going to be asked to send out our troops. This is what I do," he said. "I'm going to send out our troops to save you, so you don't have to bleed to death on the battlefield. I would do it," the colonel said. "And that is what makes me so contemptuous of [you]. Marines will die," he said, "going to get"—and he paused—"a couple of journalists."

The Friendly program was a revealing one. How should Wallace have answered? How would a twenty-first-century journalist do so? Put aside that perhaps Jennings should not have accompanied the North Kosanese soldiers at all in the midst of a war and that embedding American journalists with foreign troops at a time when they are at war with American troops plainly raises serious issues. James Fallows in his book *Breaking the News: How the Media Undermine American Democracy*, faults Wallace for not answering more thoughtfully, for not saying that in combat reporters must be above country or that they have a duty to bear impartial witness on either side, or that he had implicitly made a promise not to betray the North Kosanese when he agreed to accompany them.

A still sterner response to Wallace is difficult to avoid. He was not wrong in failing to speak more thoughtfully; it was the substance of the response itself that was disturbing. There is no fault in an American reporter reporting on a battle in which Americans are killed. Coverage of war, especially one in which Americans are involved, is not only appropriate but necessary to inform the public. And in the hypothetical (or in real life), Jennings staying silent in circumstances in which his own death was a likely result of speaking is understandable, if not markedly heroic. But for many viewers (myself included), it was difficult to accept the absence of any feeling of solidarity, of fellowship, by Wallace with the imperiled American soldiers. For him, the issue, indeed the only issue, was whether Jennings would or would not cover the story. For others, it was whether Jennings should stand mute and watch fellow Americans be killed.

Such decisions can indeed be wrenching. The notion of patriotism is used too loosely and too often to stifle controversial and sometimes valuable information or views. And far more often than not, when journalists are accused of being unpatriotic, as some viewers of Wallace wrongly concluded, it is because they are reporting truthfully about matters of genuine interest and importance. When the Pentagon Papers were published in 1971, the *New York Times* and other publications were accused by many of being unpatriotic. So was I for representing the *Times*.

When the mistreatment by American soldiers of Iraqi prisoners at the Abu Ghraib prison was revealed, journalists were accused by many people of being unpatriotic for doing so. When an American marine killed an unarmed captive in Fallujah in 2004, Edward N. Luttwak referred in an article he wrote in the *Wall Street Journal* to those journalists who revealed the information as a "pool of unpatriotic American television reporters." All of this mistakes journalism for nationalistic cheerleading along the lines that Theodore Roosevelt articulated in 1918 when he said, "There can be no fifty-fifty Americanism in this country. There is room here for only 100 percent Americanism, only for those who are Americans and nothing else."

It is easy to reject such crude flag waving, and journalists are right to do so. Yet there are situations, rare but real, in which the revelation of information could truly compromise national security or threaten lives. Even great American radicals who have treasured, advocated, and engaged in the most controversial speech have rejected this approach.

Patrick Henry, the great revolutionary firebrand, in the course of observing that "the liberties of a people never were, nor ever will be, secure, when the transactions of their rulers may be concealed from them," then added that, "transactions as relate to military operations or affairs of great consequence, the immediate promulgation of which might defeat the interests of the community, I would not wish to be published, till the end which required their secrecy should have been effected." As a whole, as Gabriel Schoenfeld, the author of *Necessary Secrets: National Secu-*

rity, the Media, and the Rule of Law, has concluded, the Framers were committed to openness, but "the fact that secrecy would on some occasions be required for purposes of assuring national security was not something they contested."

Similarly, and far more recently, Daniel Ellsberg, who has vigorously supported the conduct of Chelsea (formerly Bradley) Manning, Julian Assange, and Edward Snowden, offered this reservation in his book, *Secrets,* about leaking the Pentagon Papers: "Of course there were circumstances, such as diplomatic negotiations, certain intelligence sources and methods, or various time-sensitive military operational secrets, that warranted strict secrecy." Ellsberg acted on that view when, in giving the *New York Times* access to the Pentagon Papers case, he refrained from sharing the three volumes that dealt with negotiations to end the war for fear that it might interfere with the very process of a diplomatic resolution.

So what should we make of the following defense by Julian Assange of publishing on WikiLeaks a classified report describing radio frequency jammers used in Iraq by American soldiers to cut off signals to remotely detonated explosives? When criticized for making public such information at a time when some such jammers may still have been in use, Assange said, "WikiLeaks represents whistleblowers in the same way that lawyers represent their clients—fairly and impartially. Our 'job' is to safely and impartially conduct the whistleblower's message to the public, not to inject our own nationality or beliefs."

Everything in that statement is unpersuasive. It is one thing for WikiLeaks to seek to protect the identity of its sources but something else entirely for it to view its role as exposing any and all secrets provided by those sources, regardless of the impact of doing so. Consider the Wiki-Leaks release of a classified cable that listed sensitive facilities around the world, ranging from underseas communication lines to a laboratory in Denmark that makes a smallpox vaccine. Or its release of more than seventy-six thousand secret intelligence documents described by *Washington Post* columnist Marc A. Thiessen as exposing "the identities of at least 100 Afghans who were informing on the Taliban, including the names of their villages" and "GPS coordinates where they could be found." Or, with similar lack of care in protecting the lives of those it identified, its release of more than a quarter of a million State Department cables, apparently obtained from Chelsea Manning, which included the names of over 150 human rights whistleblowers who had been promised confidentiality. So clear was the threat to these individuals that in an unprecedented public rebuke of their own sometime source, the *New York Times,* the *Guardian, El Pais, Der Spie-gel,* and *Le Monde,* all of which had obtained documents from WikiLeaks in the past, issued a joint statement de-ploring and condemning its reckless conduct.

The issue of what information should *not* be published by entities that are dedicated to revealing information is inherently a contentious one. Reporting on matters relat-ing to national security, national defense, intelligence, and the like is essential to an informed public. The pre-sumption must always be to publish. That presumption must always mean that the arguments—and there are al-ways such arguments that can be arrayed against publica-tion, even of truthful and important information—must be resisted. And in the national security area, government officials too easily conclude that the nation's safety would be better served if hardly anything other than government press releases were published. Whether that is because they choose to shield errors of the government or them-selves, because their definition of what revelations truly hurt national security is overbroad, or because they sim-ply do not accept that there is any real public interest in the disclosure of such information, it remains important that such entreaties generally be rejected.

Only information that appears highly likely to com-promise significant national interest should be withheld.

But such information does exist. And it does sometimes come into the hands of journalists.

Consider this example. On August 2, 2013, the *New York Times* published an article revealing that the global travel alert to American citizens that had just been issued came about as a result of "intercepted electronic communications this week among senior operatives of Al Qaeda, in which the terrorists discussed attacks against American interests in the Middle East and North Africa." The *Times* in its initial article about this and CNN in its initial reporting withheld the identities of the Al Qaeda leaders whose conversations were intercepted after American intelligence officials told the journalists that publication could "jeopardize their operation."

The next day, the McClatchy Newspapers reported the names of Al Qaeda leader Ayman al-Zawahiri and Nasir al-Wuhayshi, the Yemen-based leader of Al Qaeda in the Arabian Peninsula. According to the McClatchy Washington bureau chief, James Asher, the information had been obtained in Yemen and was "pretty much common knowledge." More interesting and more disturbing was Mr. Asher's general statement. He said, "It is not unusual for CNN or the NYT to agree not to publish something because the White House asked them. And frankly, our Democracy isn't well served when journalists agree to censor their work. As I've told our readers in the past: McClatchy journalists will report fairly and independently. We will not make deals with those in power, regardless of party or philosophy."

The same day McClatchy's chief of correspondents, Mark Seibel, was quoted as saying that the information had come from Yemen and no one had asked them not to run it. He then said, "And as you know, we wouldn't be disposed to honor such a request anyway." McClatchy has deservedly received plaudits for its skeptical and too lonely reporting on the justifications for American involvement in the war in Iraq. But if McClatchy's general ongoing policy was fairly set forth in these statements, it is disturbing. To be sure, there is a certain joyous braggadocio that journalists sometimes choose to affect, a roguish take-no-prisoners, devil-may-care swagger, that has its appeal.

But if we take the McClatchy statements at face value, they are difficult to defend. Whatever the actual impact of the revelations in this case may or may not have been, the notion that it is censorship, illicit deal making, or supinely caving in to those in power simply to hear out intelligence officials, and on occasion to agree to withhold for a time publication of highly classified information that those officials had concluded could do serious harm, is hard to credit.

More persuasive as a guide is the view of Jack Fuller, the Pulitzer Prize–winning longtime editor and publisher of the *Chicago Tribune*, who summed it up this way in his book, *News Values: Ideas for an Information Age:* "When a newspaper does pierce the secrecy of government and discover information that the government has a legitimate interest in keeping secret, the reporter and editors should take those legitimate interests into account in deciding whether to publish. . . . An effort must be made to predict the consequences of disclosure and of nondisclosure. . . . Appeals by the government that the newspaper suppress the information should be listened to and not dismissed out of hand."

The issue of how journalists should treat matters related to American national security is at the heart of much of the criticism voiced by some journalists of others. Such criticism led David Carr, writing in a much-discussed piece in the *New York Times* in late 2013, to decry journalistic criticism of both Assange and Snowden. Some of Carr's thesis was persuasive. For example, the revelations of NSA snooping within the United States revealed by Snowden and the attack on journalists and other civilians in Iraq by an American Apache helicopter, first revealed by Wiki-Leaks, deserved journalistic kudos.

But Carr went further, questioning how either could

properly be condemned by American journalists at all, given the value of their revelations. As to the former, the answer is that too often WikiLeaks has simply ignored both privacy considerations—unconscionably releasing, for example, credit-card, passport, and Social Security numbers of Democratic Party donors as part of larger revelations about the conduct of that entity—as well as ones relating to national security. The distinction between Assange's approach and that of Snowden is reflected in the latter's elegant, if markedly understated, criticism of Wiki-Leaks in July 2016 for its "hostility to even modest curation" of leaked documents. Their difference in approach is illustrated by their different treatment of Snowden's revelation that American operatives had been recording all calls in the Bahamas. Glenn Greenwald, the recipient of much of the trove of Snowden's highly classified materials, determined not to reveal the identity of a second nation in which that had been done "in response to specific, credible concerns that doing so could lead to increased violence." Greenwald, who won a Pulitzer Prize for his revelations about Snowden-provided information, is a strident, persistent, even incessant critic of NSA, CIA, and other American intelligence-gathering entities and of American foreign and defense policies generally. For him to decide *not* to reveal information because of its potential dangerous impact suggests that the likelihood of harm in doing so must have seemed unambiguous. But Assange did so anyway. WikiLeaks published the name of the second nation as part of its self-described effort "to expose criminal activity by the US, having just published top secret US intercepts—US spies' reports detailing private phone calls of the presidents of France and Germany, and other senior officials, relating to internal European political and economic affairs." Editorial decisions of this sort (assuming they involved decisions at all) make it easy to conclude that for WikiLeaks, there seem to be no boundaries, no likelihood of harm, at least to American national security interests, that would lead to a decision not to publish.

The situation with Snowden is more difficult to judge. The information he possessed included material far more sensitive than anything revealed by WikiLeaks. At the same time, the decisions made by the journalists to whom he provided that information, permitting them to decide what to reveal, have taken account of the views of NSA and other national security organizations with whom they consulted.

How shall Snowden be judged? At the least, he has significantly served the nation by revealing the stunning degree to which its government engaged in surveillance of its own people. A profound national debate followed those revelations as did remedial legislation that simply would not have occurred in the absence of Snowden-provided data. He deserves great credit for doing so.

But the documents made public by Snowden revealed more than pervasive government surveillance within the United States. As noted earlier, he provided documentation that led to the public disclosure of highly classified information about American intelligence gathering abroad. The director of National Intelligence, James Clapper, has testified more broadly that "what Snowden has stolen and exposed has gone way, way beyond his professed concerns with so-called domestic surveillance programs" and that "as a result, we've lost critical foreign intelligence collection sources, including some shared with us by valued partners." Former secretary of defense Leon Panetta has asserted that the information revealed by Snowden "did damage the security that we had developed in terms of being able to track terrorists" since they "don't use the same systems anymore." House Intelligence Committee Chairman Mike Rogers has stated that Snowden's revelations have created "blind spots" in NSA surveillance by revealing US strategy to combat terrorism. If such assessments are ultimately determined to be accurate, Snowden should be judged far more harshly by the public than he has been by many.

Snowden's defenders have responded that for all the grave characterizations by government officials of the harm caused by his revelations, no specific proof has been publicly provided to support either conclusion. That is true. When VICE News filed a Freedom of Information Act request regarding any national security damage done by Snowden, 112 documents were produced, virtually all redacted. Given the nature of intelligence gathering and the continuing sensitivity of such information, one might hardly expect government officials to release the information on which they claim to be relying. But the consequence of the government failure or inability to do so is that there is little basis for the American public to pass independent judgment on the matter.

It is even more difficult to do so since knowledgeable former public officials have themselves repeatedly offered strikingly ambivalent judgments about Snowden's conduct. Former attorney general Eric Holder, who headed the Department of Justice when it filed criminal charges under the Espionage Act against Snowden for his revelations, has asserted that he "actually performed a public service for raising the debate that we engaged in." That is extraordinary, likely unprecedented praise by a prosecutor for an individual he has charged with inflicting serious harm to the national security of the nation.

Jack Goldsmith, a Harvard Law School professor and former assistant attorney general, Office of Legal Counsel and Special Counsel to the Department of Defense, has offered a similar mixed verdict. Snowden, Goldsmith concluded, "compromised scores of surveillance techniques, representing billions of dollars of investments over many years" and made it more difficult for the United States to monitor communications and access data. At the same time, Goldsmith credits Snowden for forcing the intelligence community "out of its suboptimal and unsustainable obsession with secrecy" and for raising issues that ultimately led to the adoption by Congress of the USA Freedom Act, which imposed limits on the bulk telephone metadata program of the NSA.

Given such vacillating reactions to Snowden's conduct, it simply may be too early for the American public to pass any ultimate judgment on that conduct. But it is not too soon to conclude that a number of his revelations about American intelligence gathering abroad are worthy of condemnation and not the sometimes limitless praise he has often received, particularly in Europe.

The European Parliament, the European Union's directly elected parliamentary institution, adopted a non-binding resolution on October 29, 2015, calling upon the twenty-eight EU member states to "drop any criminal charges against Edward Snowden, grant him protection and consequently prevent extradition or rendition by third parties, in recognition of his status as whistleblower and international human rights defender."

No European nation has either charged Snowden with any crime or granted him the protection advocated by the European Parliament. A review of laws relating to national security in European nations may reveal the reason for this. When political scientist Amanda L. Jacobsen, the author of an article entitled "National Security and the Right to Information in Europe," reviewed such laws in twenty European nations, she concluded that every one of them had statutes providing that public employees who had been granted access to classified national security information are subject to criminal sanctions for disclosing that information to the public and that such charges, although rare (as is the case in the United States) had been commenced in fifteen of the twenty between 1993 and 2013. In addition, persons who have not been granted authorized access to classified national security information, including journalists, may be subject to criminal penalties for disclosing that information to the public in seventeen of the twenty countries reviewed. In sixteen of the countries, the law does not favor disclosure where there is doubt about whether disclosure would harm national security.

Such decisions are often no easier for journalists to make than for courts. The memoirs of the great *New York Times* columnist James Reston reveal many decisions that he was involved in that left him uncertain scores of years later about what the *Times* should have done. He wrote that in the 1950s the *Times* was aware that the CIA was sending U-2 spy planes over the Soviet Union and determined not to publish that information, a decision Reston supported but later came to doubt. He also recalled that the *Times* was aware, before the US-funded and -directed invasion of Cuba in 1961, of the intended invasion but downplayed its story because of the imminence of the invasion, a decision that left Reston unsure forty years later of just what the paper should have done. Reston himself had criticized the then-forthcoming invasion in columns he wrote and the *Times* published before it occurred, but he remained of the view that it was, as he put it, one thing to report that the anti-Castro legions were mobilizing and quite a different thing to inform Castro of the timing of the invasion.

I had some involvement in one such matter during the Pentagon Papers case. When the hearings ended in the district court and we had prevailed, federal judge Murray Gurfein called me and a senior partner of mine into his chambers. He said to us that he wanted to talk with us "as a private citizen." The case, he said, was over, so he could talk to us in that capacity. He then said that he viewed a few of the documents he had examined in the Pentagon Papers, in particular portions of a SEATO (Southeast Asian Treaty Organization) contingency plan, as potentially dangerous to publish. He was not entering any order, he said; that was for the press to decide. But he told us that he "wished"—that was the word he used—that the *Times* would give special consideration before publishing that material.

We told him that we would advise the *Times* of his views and we did so. A decision, in fact, had already been made not to publish some of the documents. On further review the editors determined not to publish a few more and to continue to publish some others. I have always thought that was a good example of how the system ought to work.

In the Pentagon Papers case, as in most in which the Supreme Court has addressed the First Amendment, it read it broadly, expansively, in a markedly speech-protective manner. The American press has been held to have virtually carte blanche freedom to decide what to print. But that leaves the press with another decision: What to print? The First Amendment provides no answer to this question. It never does.

Index

abolitionists, 58
abortion, 14–18, 36, 83, 86
Abu Ghraib prison, 122
Active Liberty (Breyer), 18
actual malice, 51–52
Adams, John, 4, 58
advertising, 81–82, 99
Afghanistan, 125
Alito, Samuel, 17, 96, 97
All the President's Men (film), xiii
Al Qaeda, 127
American Civil Liberties Union,
  15, 98
American Pacific International
  Capital, 101
anarchists, 58
Anderson, Margaret C., 32
Animal Defenders International,
  81–83

antitrust law, 24
Archer, Jeffrey, 50
Armstrong, Lance, 50
Armstrong, William, 73
Articles of Confederation, 3
Ashcroft v. Free Speech Coalition
  (2002), 20
Asher, James, 127–28
Assange, Julian, xxi, 124–25,
  129–31
*Austin v. Michigan Chamber of
  Commerce* (1990), 110–12

Balkin, Jack, 13
Batchis, Wayne, 13
Beck, Dave, 64–65
Belgium, xvi–xvii, 42, 76–77
Bernstein, Carl, xiii
Bill of Rights, xix, 4, 5–11

Bingham, Thomas Henry, Baron
   Bingham of Cornhill, 82
Black, Hugo, vi, 11–12, 66–67, 87,
   88
Blackstone, William, 63
Bowman, Phillis, 79–80, 84
Brandeis, Louis, 15, 32
Breaking the News (Fallows), 121
Brennan, William J., 21, 22
Brennan Center, 21–22
Breyer, Stephen, 18–19, 21
Bridges v. California (1941), xx,
   63–67
Buckley v. Valeo (1976), 22, 84–86,
   96, 104, 111
Bush, George H. W., 118
Bush, Jeb, 101, 104
Byron, George Gordon Byron,
   Baron, 60

Cambridge University Press, 51
campaign finance, xx, 14, 18–19,
   36, 79–112
Canada, ix, xvi, 38–39
Cantwell, Newton, 44–45
Cantwell v. Connecticut (1940),
   44–47
Caplan, Lincoln, 24–26
Carnal Knowledge (film), 36
Caroline, princess of Monaco, 56
Carr, David, 129–30
Castro, Fidel, 136
Center for Competitive Politics,
   102
Central Intelligence Agency (CIA),
   130, 136
child pornography, 20

Christie, Chris, 104
*Citizens United v. Federal Election
   Commission* (2010), 24, 86,
   88–90, 104–5, 111–12;
   criticisms of, 83–84, 96, 97,
   100–102, 104, 108–10;
   disclosure consistent with,
   102–3, 107
civil rights movement, 36
Civil War, 58
Clapper, James, 132
clear and present danger, 66
Clinton, Bill, 55
Clinton, Hillary, 84
CNN, 127
collective speech, 19, 20, 21
commercial speech, 14, 100
conscience, freedom of, 36, 37
Constitutional Convention, 3–5,
   35
contempt of court, 63
contraception, 86
Cousins, Norman, 33
cruel and unusual punishment, 23
"crush videos," 14, 41
Cuba, 136
Curtis, Kent, 61

"dark money," 101–2, 103
Debs, Eugene V., xix
Declaration of Independence, 3
defamation, xvi, xx, 27–28, 36,
   49–54, 56
Dickinson, John, 7
disclosure requirements, 103, 107
discrimination, xvi
Douglas, William O., 12, 87–88

due process, 23
Dworkin, Ronald, 109

Ehrenfeld, Rachel, 52–53
Ellis, Joseph, 10
Ellsberg, Daniel, 124
Emerson, Thomas, 22
English law, xvii, 42, 49–53, 59,
    66–67
equality, xvi
Eritrea, 37–38
Espionage Act (1917), 28, 57, 133
European Convention on Human
    Rights, xvii, 80
European Court of Human Rights,
    xvii, 42, 55, 56, 80–83, 84
European Court of Justice, 69
European Parliament, 134–35
European Union, 69–70, 76

Facebook, 37
Fallows, James, 121
false advertising, 99
Federal Communications
    Commission (FCC), 102–3
Federal Elections Commission
    (FEC), 92
Federalist, 7
Fineman, Howard, 109
fines, 24
Finland, 55
First World War, xix
flag burning, 13, 20, 36
Ford, Gerald, 118
Four Freedoms, xxiii
Fourth Amendment, 26
France, 54

Frankfurter, Felix, 67
Freedom of Speech (Rockwell), xxiii
Fried, Charles, xv
Friendly, Fred, 117–18
Fuller, Jack, 129
Funding Evil (Ehrenfeld), 52

Gawker, 57
Germany, 47–48, 54, 56
Ginsburg, Ruth Bader, 18
Goldman, William, xiii
Goldsmith, Jack, 134
Google, xvii, 37, 69–72, 76, 77
Gora, Joel, 98
Greenberg, Maurice, 101
Greenwald, Glenn, 130
Guardian (newspaper), xxii, 70, 126
Gurfein, Murray, 136–37

Hale, Brenda, Baroness Hale of
    Richmond, 82
Hamilton, Alexander, 6–7
Hand, Augustus, 60
Hasen, Richard L., 109
hate speech, xvi–xvii, xix–xx, 39,
    47–49
Heap, Jane, 32
Henry, Patrick, 5–6, 123
Hill v. Colorado (2000), 14–18
Hogan, Hulk, 57
Holder, Eric, 133
Holmes, Kennan, 65
Holmes, Oliver Wendell, 32,
    62–64, 65–67
Holocaust denial, 47–48
House Un-American Activities
    Committee, 58

Index

Ignatius, David, 102
independent expenditures, 14,
86–87
India, 48–49
Industrial Workers of the World,
30
Internal Revenue Service (IRS),
102, 103
International Covenant on Civil
and Political Rights (1966), 44
International Press Institute,
53–54
Internet, 117
Iraq, 124
Issacharoff, Samuel, 48–49

Jackson, Robert H., 11
Jacobsen, Amanda L., 135
Jefferson, Thomas, 3, 4, 5
Jennings, Peter, 118–20, 121–22
Joyce, James, 32

Kagan, Elena, 19, 91–93
Kennedy, Anthony, 12, 16–17, 84,
88–90, 104–5, 110
Kernochan, Frederic, 32
Koch brothers, 103
Korean War, 116

labor unions, 14, 64, 86, 89, 91
League of Conservation Voters,
103
Lewinsky, Monica, 55
libel, xx, 27–28, 36, 49–53, 56
Liberace, 50
Lincoln, Abraham, 112
Lincoln, James, 6

Little Review, 32
Lord of the Rings (Tolkien), 74
Luttwak, Edward N., 122–23

Madison, James, 3, 4, 5, 8–10, 37
Madison's Music (Neuborne),
23–24
Maher, Bill, 44
Mahfouz, Khalid bin, 52–53
Malicious Communications Act
(1988), 42–43
Manjoo, Farhad, 71
Manning, Chelsea (Bradley), 124,
125
McCarthy, Joseph, 58
McClatchy Newspapers, 127–28
McConnell, Mitch, 84, 109, 111
McCullen v. Coakley (2014), 17
McCutcheon v. Federal Election
Commission (2014), 18–19
McDonnell, Robert, 105
McInerney, James, 32
McNamara, Robert, 113
media companies, 89, 96–97
Medvedev, Dmitry, 115
Merkel, Angela, 115
Miami Herald Publishing Co. v.
Tornillo (1974), 94, 96
Mills v. Alabama (1966), 93–96
Monroe, James, 8
Moss, Joseph, 32
Murphy, Frank, 87
Muslims, 41–43

National Rifle Association, 98, 103
national security, 28, 116–17,
123–37

National Security Agency (NSA),
129, 131, 134
Nebraska Press Association v. Stuart
(1976), 28
Necessary Secrets (Schoenfeld),
123–24
Neuborne, Burt, 23–24
newspapers: ownership of, 89,
96–97; right-to-reply require-
ments imposed on, 94, 95
News Values (Fuller), 129
New York Society for the
Suppression of Vice, 32
New York Times, 99–100, 103, 127;
Citizens United decried by,
96–98, 100, 108; national
security and, 116–17, 125–26,
127, 135–36; Pentagon Papers
published by, 113–14, 115, 122,
124; political contributions by,
101
New York Times Company v. Sullivan
(1964), 51
Nicol, Andrew, 50
Nike v. Kasky (2003), 98–99
Nixon, Richard, xiii
North Korea, 37–38
Norway, 57

Obama, Barack, 52, 58, 109–10
obscenity, 27–28, 36, 59–60
Ogletree, Charles, 118–20
Olbermann, Keith, 109
Orwell, George, xxi–xxii

pamphlets, 92, 93
Panetta, Leon, 132

Patterson, Paul, 60–62
Patterson v. Colorado (1907), 60–64,
65
Pearl Harbor, 116
Pentagon Papers, xxii, 28, 113–14,
115, 117, 122, 124, 136–37
perjury, 27
Perry, Rick, 104
Planned Parenthood, 103
Poland, 43
political action committees (PACs),
90, 101, 103
Political Censorship (Goldstein), 29
political speech, 88
post–Civil War amendments, xiv,
23
Powe, Lucas, Jr., 62
pretrial publicity, 28
prior restraint, 28, 62
prisoners, 57
prisons, 24
privacy, xvi, xviii, xx, 15, 56–57
Profumo, John, 50
public officials, 51, 54
Putin, Vladimir, 51

Quinn, John, 32

Randolph, Edmund, 7
Regina v. Hicklin (1868), 59–60
religion: disparagement of,
xvi–xvii, 43, 44–47, 48–49; free
exercise of, xix, 11, 35, 38,
39–40, 44–47
Reporters without Borders,
37, 55
Reston, James, 136

"right to be forgotten," xviii, xx, 69–77
right to counsel, 86
Roberts, John G., 12, 21, 41, 90, 92
Robertson, Geoffrey, 49–50
Rockwell, Norman, xxiii
Rogers, Mike, 132
Roosevelt, Franklin D., xxii–xxiii, 116
Roosevelt, Theodore, 123
Rosenfeld, Michel, 47–48
Rossiter, Clinton, 3–4
Rousseff, Dilma, 115
Rusbridger, Alan, xxii
Rutledge, Wiley, 87
Ruusunen, Susan, 55

Sanders, Bernie, 104, 106
San Francisco Chronicle, 101, 108
Saturday Review of Literature, 33
Scalia, Antonin, 15–16, 17–18, 91–92, 110, 111–12
Schoenfeld, Gabriel, 123–24
Scott, A. A., 65
Scowcroft, Brent, 118
search and seizure, 23, 26
Secrets (Ellsberg), 124
Sedition Act (1798), 57–58
Seibel, Mark, 128
Shannon, Matthew, 65
Shelley, Percy Bysshe, 60
Sherman, Roger, 4–5, 7
Sixth Amendment, 86
slavery, 23
Snowden, Edward, xxi, xxii, 114–15, 124, 129–35
Snyder v. Phelps (2011), 21, 40

socialists, xix, 58
"social welfare" organizations, 102
Society for the Protection of the Unborn Child, 79–81
Sotomayor, Sonia, 19
SPEECH Act (2010), 53
Starr, C. V., and Company, 101
Stevens, John Paul, 12, 15, 89, 97, 110
Stewart, Malcolm, 90–91, 92–93
Stewart, Potter, 28
Sullivan, Kathleen, 26–27
Summer, John S., 32

Taft-Hartley Act (1947), 86–87
Taliban, 125
Telegraph (newspaper), 72–76
Thiessen, Marc A., 125
Thomas, Clarence, 15–16, 17
Tolkien, J. R. R., 74
Tribe, Laurence, 18
Truman, Harry S., 87
Trump, Donald J., xvii, 43, 106

Ulysses (Joyce), xix, 32, 60
US Chamber of Commerce, 103
United States v. Auto Workers (1957), 87–88
United States v. CIO (1948), 87
United States v. Stevens (2009), 41

Vice News, 133
Vietnam War, 113, 115
Volokh, Eugene, 86

Walker, Scott, 103–4
Wallace, Mike, 118, 120, 121–22

Warren, Earl, 88
Washington Post, 100–101, 108, 115
Webster, Noah, 7–8
Westboro Baptist Church, 21,
    39–40
Westmoreland, William, 118
Whatcott, William, 38–39
Whitman, James Q., 54
WikiLeaks, 125–26, 130, 131

Wilson, Woodrow, 58
Woodward, Bob, xiii
Woolsey, James, 60
World War I, 58
Wu, Tim, 25–26, 59
Wuhayshi, Nasir al-, 127

Zawahiri, Ayman al, 127
Zola, Émile, 59–60